G

Ben Delaney's
Nonprofit Marketing Handbook

© 2018 Ben Delaney, CyberEdge Information Services

Ebook ISBN: 978-1-5136-3555-2
Paperbound ISBN: 978-1-5136-3554-5
Library of Congress Control Number: 2018906090

To order additional copies of this book,
please visit Amazon or contact the publisher:

CyberEdge Information Services, Oakland, CA USA
510 419-0800
www.BenDelaney.com
NPMH@BenDelaney.com
@BenDelaneyNow
www.linkedin.com/in/BenDelaney

Cover and interior design by Ck Kuebel Design: www.kuebel.com

Ben Delaney's
Nonprofit Marketing Handbook

The hands-on guide to communications and marketing in nonprofit organizations

By Ben Delaney

Acknowledgements

Thanks to...

Debbie Bardon, who thought I could lead and grow a social enterprise.

Kathy Cole of West Wind Consulting for helping me better understand important aspects of nonprofit messaging.

John Griffin, who, as Publisher of PC WORLD, introduced me to market research and statistical analysis.

Carol Soker Hunt, of Carol Soker & Associates, taught me everything I know about media and how one buys and evaluates it.

Michael Hunt did the proofreading on the first edition. If anything is still wrong, it's because I didn't do what he suggested. My bad. Michael has left us and is greatly missed.

Daniel Kennedy of Daniel Kennedy Communications opened many doors for me, and offered many important tips on how to make public and press relations work for an organization.

Ck Kuebel, for her valuable assistance in editing the manuscript, frequent suggestions for content and presentation, and for the excellent graphic design she provides to keep me looking my best.

Gerd Meissner has provided a whole host of valuable tips and tricks and has been an invaluable sounding board for many of the ideas in this book.

Ray Schaaf, who was the first to trust me with a Marketing Director title.

Armando Zumaya, who taught me everything I know about fundraising and development, as well as some important lessons on diplomacy.

Philip Arca, Tobias Beckwith, Jan Cohen, and Kathy Looper all read parts of this new edition and provided valuable insights and suggestions.

Thanks also to the many reviewers who showed me once again that LinkedIn is an incredible community. They provided valuable input and insight that have made this a much better book.

And to the many others who have helped me on my journey, selflessly sharing their love and knowledge, and showing me that you don't need a fortune to change someone's life for the better.

Table of Contents

Building a Successful Nonprofit MarCom Program

About this book

There are more than a million nonprofit organizations in the United States. Every one of them needs to tell its story, find clients, solicit donations, sell services, and encourage its volunteers. Yet few have a marketing department, and many face serious challenges in meeting their communications and marketing goals.

When I was hired to be the first ever marketing and communications director for a San Francisco nonprofit engaged in public school reform, I searched Amazon and my local bookstores for a guidebook. With more than 30 years of marketing experience, I was comfortable that I knew my craft – but I wanted some counsel on what marketing and communications (MarCom) was like in the nonprofit world. I was terribly disappointed. The few books available that addressed the issue were dry as dust – academic tomes that seemed to be a hundred years old. Still, I bought the most-praised. And was I ever frustrated. The author, authoritative, knowledgeable and didactic, struck a note of ivory-tower purity that had little in common with the down and dirty, hectic, pressure-filled, and deadline dependent world of marketing in which I had worked for so many years. And indeed, when I started my new job I found that marketing in a nonprofit was a lot like the work I had done for dozens of high-tech companies and startups. It was not dry and dead. It was full of life, replete with exacting requirements, personality issues, cultural sensitivities, and impossible deadlines.

After I left that job, ironically the victim of my own successes (I couldn't convince them to raise prices on their events and services, and so, the more seats I filled the more money they lost.), I decided that I could help the next me, the nonprofit MarCom initiate, by sharing what I have learned and summarizing what that person needs to do, and how to do it successfully in the nonprofit environment.

Addressed to the MarCom manager in small to medium sized nonprofits, this book assumes that the reader has little formal knowledge of marketing. In plain language, it provides a hands-on reference that can be referred to frequently, providing checklists and actionable tips to make marketing easier and more effective. In this Second Edition, I have updated information that was out of date, and added a brief discussion and a table of resources for marketing automation. In addition, there is a new chapter on a critical aspect on nonprofit MarCom – Crisis Communications Management (page 137). Finally, this edition is fully indexed to make it easier to use.

I start by comparing cultures and continue through the basic concepts, tools, and processes that ensure success in nonprofit MarCom. I offer tips on choosing marketing tools and how to use them effectively. I conclude with a glossary, and index, and additional resources for the nonprofit marketing team.

I hope you find this helpful. Let me know at npmh@bendelaney.com.

1

Introduction:
System Marketing™ Your Key to Success

Why integrating communications into every activity gives you way more bang for the buck.

System Marketing™ means that your marketing is a system, in the same way that your financial procedures form a system. In either case, the specific task is aware of, and is informed by, the total organization. Everything affects everything – it's all connected.

System Marketing directs that you align your goals, procedures, and communications to all pull in the same direction, with verbal, nonverbal, electronic, and print messages, and staff attitudes, all reinforcing the same message. It ensures that everyone in the organizations is speaking with one voice.

Most importantly, System Marketing requires a deep understanding of the marketplace and the customer, and the ability to address the customer's expressed, implied and inferred needs and desires. This requires research. That research may be as simple as a comment sheet on your front counter, or as complex as a multivariate, blind, controlled test. The cost typically varies with the number of words used to describe the research.

For example, putting a comment sheet on your front counter requires nothing more than a piece of paper, a pen, and some Scotch tape. It will result in some of your customers providing valuable insights into your operation at minimal expense. The multivariate, blind, controlled test will probably take several people several months, will require a series of letters after the authors' names, will result in a colorful bound report with footnotes, and will cost appropriately. In either case, when research is done thoughtfully and with well-defined goals, it is almost always worth the money.

Let me give you an example of how research helps. A while back I was asked to provide a campaign to increase interest in and visits to a nice retirement home in Marin County, California. As I talked with the staff, I realized that they had only the vaguest of ideas about why people chose to live there, or not. So we started asking some questions.

First we conducted a written survey of the current residents, asking them what they liked about living there, along with a few other questions. We also asked where they had lived before. From this we gained a lot of insight. As expected, people liked the beautiful grounds and that it was easy to get into town for shopping. The food was good, as were interactions with the staff. What surprised us was the most important factor in the move-in decision: People who lived there really liked that they could bring their own furniture!

We then sent out a postal mailing to a large population. I don't remember the exact number, but we mailed to more than 10,000 people over age 55, within a 40 mile radius of the facility. Why 40 miles? Because that's average maximum distance from which residents had come. Some had come from farther, but more than 80% had previously lived within 40 miles.

The mailing included a brochure illustrated with professional photos, taken on the grounds, of people who actually lived there, sporting the headline, "Come Home to the [Facility]". We emphasized the hot-button items we knew about from the survey: just like home, extra secure and safe, bring your favorite furniture, close to your friends and family, and a familiar landscape.

This became the most successful direct mail effort I have ever done. We received a 24% response rate, and a 10% conversion rate, thereby beating expectations by a mile, and filling the waiting list. I am convinced that the research set the tone that enabled this successful effort. But equally important was the participation and buy-in of the staff, the truthfulness of the messaging, and the ability of the intake staff to model exactly what people expected. That's System Marketing at work!

System Marketing in your organization

Your organization can establish System Marketing as SOP (Standard Operating Procedure). Do the research needed to truly know your customers, the marketplace, and the outside factors that impact that marketplace. Share staff knowledge about current customer-facing processes and communications. Listen to complaints, and don't dismiss them as trivial. Be sure everybody is involved and heard. Review your mission, vision, objectives and impact statement to be sure they are current and actually reflect what you do and want to do, and how it happens.

Then you can unify communications and attitudes. Attitudes are important because a large part of your customer and prospect communications is old fashioned conversation, as well as emails and other personal interaction. It is essential that everyone understands and buys in to the official message, and is able to reflect it in every action and utterance including answering the phone, responding to an email, completing a proposal, talking at the bar at a conference: the language, style, and talking points should all reinforce your messaging. That message is strengthened by consistent usage, including your website, logos, business cards, brochures, and advertising. When all of this is synchronized, then you have a marketing system and System Marketing.

Frankly, I don't consider this rocket science. I have been thinking about it for a long time and have seen the theory proven. Much of this is common sense, and just plain good business, be it for- or nonprofit. This book breaks down various marketing tasks and offers suggestions on how and when to use them. Regardless of the marketing mix you choose, when you keep System Marketing in mind all of your marketing will be more effective.

2

How Your Nonprofit is Just Like a Hot Internet Startup

There are more similarities than you might expect.

People frequently ask me how I went from high-tech marketing to the nonprofit world. Actually, I don't see that much difference between the two environments. They have a lot in common. High-tech companies and nonprofit organizations share many characteristics and face similar challenges. That means that a good marketer, after learning the important aspects of an organization – like programs, products, services, and culture – can handle a nonprofit's needs as easily as those of a high-tech startup.

Here are a few of the things that nonprofits and high-tech companies have in common:

Mission driven: Have you noticed how high-tech marketers often have titles like "guru" or "evangelist"? That's because just like nonprofits, high-tech startups are driven by their mission, with the excitement and the compulsion to get their message out – a message of new hope and opportunities presented by new technologies. Nonprofits are driven by similar goals; to ensure that the right people hear their important message of needs and hopes. This is a basic factor in communications for both constituencies. Many of the same techniques, carefully tailored to the needs of the organization and the expectations of the audience, will work in either type of organization.

Led by a brilliant, inspired leader: The engineer who invented the technology still heroically leads the company. The Executive Director, brilliant in her understanding of the issues, people, and connections at the nexus of the cause, is the go-to voice on her area of expertise. High-tech and nonprofits, led by really smart people, often lack basic Marketing and Communications (MarCom) skills. Both types of organizations need strong MarCom leadership and often lack that expertise.

Limited funds: Even the hottest venture-capital funded tech startups have to make money, or they end up dumping all those cool Aeron chairs on eBay. Nonprofits are chronically under-funded. There are many smart, low-cost marketing techniques that can quickly help the bottom line.

Need for strong branding: Every organization needs a strong brand. Brands help establish a comfortable, family-like relationship. Think about the Girl Scouts, Nike, The American Cancer Society, Google, or the Salvation Army. Each of those brands hold meaning for a lot of people, and because of that familiarity half of the communications job is already done. New company – new cause; both need the same thing: a strong brand that elicits warm feelings in the heart of the organization's constituency.

Unsure of the value of marketing: When funds are limited, not every good idea can be followed up. Some projects get done today, some are put off, some are canceled. Often the first casualty of financial constraints is the MarCom budget line. That is a huge mistake. When an organization is small, or is dealing with a setback, or has a great new opportunity, marketing helps make good things happen. Marketing doesn't have to cost a lot, and it should be treated as an investment, with goals, milestones, and a return on investment (ROI).

Need for accountability in marketing: Every organization needs to keep its eyes on the ball of accountability. Marketing results can and should be measured. How many people responded to a mailing? Were they the people we were hoping to hear from? Did our ad bring in the number of inquiries we expected? Does our website provide good quality leads? Are people retweeting our tweets? Those kinds of questions matter in every organization.

So you see, the nonprofit world isn't that different from that of high-tech startups. The same time-tested marketing tools (frequently upgraded as technology changes) help any organization that is trying to make the world a better place. While the objectives of a high-tech company will be completely different from those of a nonprofit, the same tools work to get the message out. An advertisement can sell disc drives or encourage donors. A press release can announce the latest version of the Gizmotron, or let people know that the millionth child has been saved. You can do either.

After decades of selling Gizmotrons, I can assure you that it feels really good to be working to educate children, save the environment, stamp out poverty and disease, or encourage peace.

3

Some Best Practices for Nonprofit Marketing

There's a lot to learn from the marketing pros

My first few months in the nonprofit environment were a real eye-opening period. I felt confident that I knew my craft, but I had a lot to learn about the culture and work style of the nonprofit (NP) environment. Though they were sometimes tough, the lessons I learned have helped me going forward. But I recognized that there were a few things that NP organizations can learn from the private sector.

In particular, the best practices of marketing that are routinely applied in the for-profit (FP) world can provide useful structure for the NP marketer, in large or small organizations. MarCom is essential to nonprofits, for getting people to events, encouraging donors, and even selling products. System Marketing is especially important for nonprofits, because it enables the leveraging of all MarCom efforts.

Let's look at a few of the MarCom best practices that have a place in the NP world. The next chapter adds some more.

Responsibility and the collaborative decision-making process.

In a democracy, everyone has an opportunity to speak. Each citizen gets a vote. Each vote is of equal value. After a count of votes, decisions are made.

Most businesses are not democracies. Most businesses are run by (hopefully benign) dictators, who have virtual life and death power. Decisions can be made quickly, and responsibility for bad decisions is usually obvious.

Many NPs are run more like democracies than most FP organizations. In NPs, staff meetings are held regularly, departments and various groups meet frequently. Everyone has a say. And depending on the leadership style of the top person, decisions are made by consensus. Often, decision-making is a long, laborious process as the leadership struggles to create consensus. Responsibility for bad decisions is shared, because everybody bought in, or at least, had a say.

However, in an efficient business somebody has to be in charge. Somebody has to watch the budget and deadlines, and ensure that the work is being done, correctly, on time, and at the right price. Each project needs one (and one only) accountable manager.

Once a decision is made, make one person responsible for its correct execution.

Accountability

Some organizations see their marketing budget as a witch's cauldron. They throw money in, and magic happens. Many a manager has complained to me that he was spending his marketing budget, and making sales, but he had no idea what he was getting for his money. Hearing this always makes me cringe. This is the manager who, when times get tough is going to cut the marketing budget to save money. That should seldom happen. Marketing is an investment, not an expense. And like any investment, it needs to be closely monitored and managed. And by the way, many studies show that in tough times, the companies that continue marketing emerge much stronger than those that cut marketing.

Accountability in marketing is not just a slogan. It is a necessity. Each program should include goals, a budget, milestones, deadlines, and a post-action debrief.

If you are leading a team, do your best to get the right people on that team: people, be they staff or vendors, who will do what they promise, when they say they will. Be proactive about getting the other resources you need to do the job properly. Set reasonable expectations, so that people undedrstand what their roles and responsibilities are, and the schedule of the project.

Accountability in marketing is based on measurable goals like: We expect between 1000 and 2000 leads from this mailing; This ad will produce 200 leads and five new customers; This program will bring us between $200,000 and $500,000 in new pledges; We expect this press release to result in two national stories and ten regional articles; or This campaign will bring us 10 new major donors, 20 renewals, and 200 new, smaller donors. These are measurable goals.

Every well-planned MarCom effort includes anticipated results. Every campaign should also feature a full-team, post-campaign debrief in which you look at how well the process went, the results of the effort, and how to do it better the next time. Obviously, efforts that don't meet expectations need to be looked at closely to see why you missed your estimated return.

Marketing is a repetitive endeavor. Even an effort that provides better-than-expected results should be looked at to see how you exceeded your goals, and to determine if it was a fluke or replicable.

Remember, while there is an art to marketing, most of it is science.

Test, test, test

How do you know what's best in marketing and communications? You test, test, test.

MarCom testing is the research that makes MarCom a science. You can test message, demographic selections, imagery, different media, and different options within a type of media. You do this testing by setting up small, controlled experiments, and evaluating the results.

Testing is so important that I devote an entire chapter (Chapter 15, page 96) to it. Stay tuned.

You (often) get what you pay for

Volunteers, and the hazard of the lowest bidder.
Volunteers are great if they can do the job you need done. Remember, though, to balance cost versus benefits. Because MarCom is such a strategic function in the organization, the use of volunteers has to be carefully planned. For example, I think nearly anyone can stuff envelopes properly. But I want a skilled professional designing my website, or writing a press release.

Also, I generally advise against using a lowest-bidder budgeting plan. If your vendors are bidding too low, they may not be making enough money to provide support when you need it. It's important to build a reliable team of vendors, so that when you get in a deadline bind, they are willing to help you. Low bidders have less loyalty. All else being equal, I typically prefer a low to middle bid.

There are plenty of other best practices in nonprofit MarCom. The next chapter will give you four more.

4

A Few More Best Practices of Nonprofit MarCom

In which we continue our discussion of some of the best practices in marketing for nonprofits, with a focus on PR.

Marshall McLuhan was right.

In many cases, the medium is the message. Be sure you match the media to the audience.

How long have you had your email address? Two years? Ten? Do you subscribe to a daily newsfeed? How do you keep up with your social community: telephone, email, text messaging, hand-written notes?

How you answer those questions show your preference for media. You are part of several demographic groups, each of which has different preferences and habits. Why should you care? Because if you send a CD-ROM full of multimedia to an older newspaper subscriber, he's likely to use your disc for a coaster. Likewise, if you send a 16-page brochure to a Millennial, it may just be filed under "recyclable."

The other aspect of this is that you need to match your media to your message. A long policy discussion is best presented on paper. But an emotional pitch for donors to help solve a chronic problem might best be made on video. The great speech your Executive Director made to the local Rotary Club would make a fine podcast. An urgent request for donations to lobby Congress is definitely best as email. Trying to understand the opinions of your constituents may best be done with Facebook or Twitter. It's essential in these days of multiple media and multiple information gathering styles that you use the appropriate media to reach the people who need to hear your message.

Balancing mission and MarCom

Crassly commercial. Unethical. Snake oil salesmen. Only interested in the money.

I have heard marketers called all of this and worse. But marketing is not evil. Even the purest mission-driven organization needs to let people know what's up. No matter how valiant your cause, your landlord wants the rent every month. Nonprofits need money and their MarCom efforts help keep it flowing.

As a nonprofit marketer, you need to be especially sensitive to the onus of commercialism. You need to keep the mission and vision in the forefront as you get your messages out. Even if you are selling T-shirts and mugs with pictures of a cute seal pup on them, you need to stress how this purchase benefits the cause, and let your buyers feel good about your organization while they support it.

This point is especially important for people moving from the commercial world to nonprofits. If you are in this situation, remember to stay cool. Downplay the competitive aspect of your personality and your messaging. Keep the mission firmly in front, and don't ever bash the competition.

Likewise, if you have always been working for the public good, remember that these days people are overwhelmed by commercial messages, news, and noise. You need good marketing and communications to get your message to the people. Your good work will go for naught if you can't find the support you need. Nonprofits need marketing as much as any hot internet startup.

Is it news?

Everybody loves to see their name in the paper. Service organizations are no exception. But making news and being sure it has an upbeat appeal is not as simple as it may seem.

Journalists are bombarded with press releases. When I was editing a small technical magazine, I often got 20 to 50 press releases a week. Editors at major publications might get 100 a day. I could use about six a month. Do the math and you'll understand how tough it is to break through to publications.

There are at least ten factors that are key to getting your news in front of readers and viewers. Keep these items in mind.

1: **Write well.** I can assure you that nothing turns off an editor more than a poorly written release. If you are sending your release in English, be certain that your writer knows English. And grammar. And syntax. Know when to use "your" and "you're. " Be careful about "there," they're" and "their." Avoid colloquialisms, slang, and jargon, except for special impact. Check the spelling. If you're not a good writer, find someone who is and ask for their help. Finally, before you send out your news release, read it aloud to check for flow.

2: **Spell correctly.** I'm not that picky, but a press release with misspellings drives me crazy. Be especially careful of people and place names. Run the spelling checker. Then give it to your pickiest colleague to proofread, because spell check software can make some stunning mistakes

3: **Invest in the *AP Stylebook* and *Elements of Style*.** These are essential in any writer's library. Read them and always have them handy when you are writing a news release.

4: **Targeting: do your homework.** Another pet peeve of editors is getting releases that have nothing to do with what they cover (their beat). Every week I got releases on cosmetics (don't care), new financial products (boring), and breakthrough labor saving devices (sorry, too tired to read that). The simplest research is to go to the media websites of the publications to which you plan to send your release, and go to the staff page. Most will tell you who covers what beat. If they don't, look through some articles until you find the editor or reporter who covers your type of organization or product. That person may care. No one else will.

5: **Pick up the phone.** Journalists are people, too. They like to know with whom they are dealing, and they are more responsive to people and organizations they know. So after you have done your research, pick up the phone and call the journalists you have identified as potentially interested in your organization. Ask them what they cover and how they like to get information. Invite them to events. Send them some background material. Make your Executive Director (ED) available for background interviews (after coordinating calendars). Do what a friend would do – be helpful. A caution: Don't overdo it, or you may end up on the permanent black list. Media people are wary, knowing that their publications are highly desired forums. So stay in touch, but don't push too hard.

6: **Make it real.** Another issue I have with many

companies is that their releases aren't actually news , or even interesting. Be sure you really have something to say. An internal promotion to a mid-level position is not generally newsworthy. A new top-level person is interesting. A big grant award will catch eyeballs. Setting a record, rolling out an important new program, giving away a million dollars – those are all newsworthy.

7: **What's the subject?** If you're sending your release by email, be sure to use a subject line that makes sense. Don't get carried away and don't make a sales pitch. A subject like, "'New XYZ Foundation Program Feeds 10,000 Starving Children" is more likely to get the release read than, "Gala Event Ends Child Hunger." Believable and interesting are the two key concepts to remember.

8: **Make it local.** Few news stories are of national import. Do your research to discover who covers your kind of news in areas where it really matters. A new after-school program in Stockton is most interesting to people in Stockton. A grant to the Trenton Theater Association may not play well in New York City. Keep your geography in mind when you send your releases.

9: **Keep it short.** Journalists seldom read long releases. If they need more they'll ask for it. Enough said.

10: **Don't send attachments.** In these days of rampant computer viruses, spyware, trojans, and other maladies, few journalists will open attachments from unknown correspondents. Put your release, in plain text, in the body of an email. If a reporter needs a different format, she'll ask.

There are plenty of other good ideas about how to create and execute good marketing and communications in nonprofits, but, those are the top items on my list on MarCom best practices. Keep them in mind and you won't go wrong.

5

Using Social Media Well

For several years now, people have been talking about the importance of social media. But it seems that a few people, and even fewer organizations, really know how to use this medium.

Facebook, LinkedIn, Pinterest, Twitter, Tumblr, Flicker, Instagram, Google+ — it seems the list is endless. We all hear about the great successes that some people have had with social media, but the reality is, going viral on Twitter is as about as likely as winning the lottery. Sure, Justin Bieber has 106,372,993 followers (April 2018). But the likelihood of your organization getting close to that number is slim.

One thing to remember is that social media primarily reaches the people you already know. That makes the challenge one of getting people that you know to sign up for your social media. It's a chicken and egg situation: If you don't already know someone, how do you tell them about your social media?

It may surprise you that many people are introduced to social media through conventional media. Most commonly, this is through the very oldest form of human communication – talking. Yes, people still talk to each other, telling their friends and acquaintances about their Twitter accounts, urging them to like them on Facebook, talking about shared photos on Pinterest. This works. If you use social media, it's likely that you got started due to a recommendation from a friend or colleague.

Obviously, this is a slow way to build up a following. I doubt that Justin knows 106 million people. So how did he do it? He did it with various techniques that you can follow and emulate.

Here are my 12 tips for social media success in your System Marketing regime.

1. **Follow**: Follow people and organizations that you find interesting. They'll see you, and some will follow you in return.

2. **Lead**: Post original ideas and thoughts. Express yourself and take a stand. People want to know what you think, and they will follow you if you have interesting things to say.

3. **Make news**: Give people scoops on stuff. Talk about the first, the best, the most interesting. Don't wait for others – if it's important to you, it's important.

4. **Report news:** Tell about things that no one else is talking about. Talk about the great things you and your organization are doing. Report on local events

the mainstream news doesn't cover. It's the internet age, we are all content creators.

5. **Entertain**: A little humor makes your posts more interesting and fun. Surprise people and make them laugh and they'll come back for more.

6. **Inform:** Talk about what you know well. People are hungry for good sources of reliable information. If you are expert in something, tell people how it works.

7. **Be there:** Don't be a stranger. Nothing is older than a month-old tweet. Be sure you can maintain your social media with new content at least two or three times every week. It's better not to start if you can't keep going. People will lose interest fast if your content is stale.

8. **Connect**: Be sure that all of your online presences are connected. Put social media buttons on your website, your email, your signs and your print ads. Use QR codes to send mobile users to your sites. Every medium has its place, and that place is connected to every other medium you use.

What are QR Codes?

Quick Response, or QR, codes are pixilated boxes that encode information like website addresses and contact info. It's like a bar code, but can be read very quickly and has greater storage capacity. QR codes are especially handy to provide links to mobile devices, and are created at no charge on a number of websites. Your phone or tablet may have a reader app, and many current cameras will read these codes. If not the apps are free and easy to use. Get yours on iTunes or the Play Store. Here's a QR code example.

9. **Share**: Tell everybody about everything. Talk about the great things your partners are doing. Mention grants you've received and the projects you're working on. Ask for volunteers. Share your vendors and the people you love to work with. Share tips for fixing things, getting the best stuff, and making great deals. The more you share, the more people will want to know.

10. **Promote**: Tell the world. Your social media is worth the time. It's exciting! It's fun. It's timely and interesting! In fact, you can't live without it! Use every media opportunity to promote your social media. Talk about it, put it in brochures, mention it in print ads and be certain to cross promote all of your media. You don't know where your next follower may be lurking – be sure she gets the message.

11. **Dialogue**: Social media is a two-way street. Answer comments and thank people for retweeting or favoriting your postings. Share info on Facebook and LinkedIn to increase the number of people who know of you. Don't just sit there – engage!

12. **# & @:** On Twitter and Facebook, you can use a hash tag (# symbol) to indicate a cross reference. Anything with a # in front of it, like #NPMktngBook, becomes a searchable item. Your tweets and postings will be seen more if you include hashtags in them. The @ sign indicates another account on Twitter. For example, I am @BenDelaneyNow. If you include these handles in your tweets, the people you reference are informed, and are more likely to check you out. By the way, don't overdo it. A recent study of Twitter found that the optimum number of hash tags is two or three. Fewer or more than that tend to be ignored.

Be sure you don't forget traditional media, but be equally certain that social media are in your promotional mix. Remember, optimizing media to reach your audience with the message you want them to get is both a science and an art. As such, pay attention to the research, and use all the tools at your disposal.

Marketing automation (MA) is the use of software tools to do some routine marketing tasks. For example, when your web form is submitted, you MA software can send an email to the submitter, enter the data in your CRM system, and inform you of the event.

Here are a few of the MA tools available. There are many more, and the list changes every week, so explore, experiment, and discover the best tools to get your job done more efficiently.

Email Management Systems
(Costs are minimum per month for 10,000 contacts)

Product	URL	Functions	Notes	$/Mo
Constant Contact	www.constantcontact.com	Primarily mass email for marketing	Discount for prepayment	$95
Mail Chimp	www.mailchimp.com	Primarily mass email for marketing	Many connections to other apps	$75
Vertical Response	www.verticalresponse.com	Primarily mass email for marketing	Substantial NP discount.	$83

System Integration/Connection Software
Used to connect many types of apps to each other.

Product	URL	Functions	Notes	$/Mo
IFTTT	www.ifttt.com	Connector for many applications	Provides many preconfigured connections, allows users to build more. Connects to many popular online apps.	Free
Zapier	www.zapier.com	Connector for many applications	Provides many preconfigured connections, allows users to build more. Connects to many popular online apps. Limited free version.	$20

Marketing Automation Systems
(Costs are minimum per month for 10,000 contacts)

Product	URL	Functions	Notes	$/Mo
Aritic	www.aritic.com	SEO, forms, email, audience segmentation, analysis, connects to CRM	Very similar to Marketo functionally. PinPoint (email) only	$299
Hubspot	www.hubspot.com	SEO, forms, email, audience segmentation, analysis, connects to CRM (included at no cost)	Includes CRM system as hub. Add "Marketing" (Inbound lead handling), "Sales" (lead management), and/or "Customers" (coming soon) Starter prices.	$100
Marketo	www.marketo.com	SEO, forms, email, audience segmentation, analysis, connects to CRM	#1 rated. Used by big orgs. Lots of functions. Steep learning curve.	$999
ZOHO	www.zoho.com	CRM, accounting, email, app development platform, help desk, HR, G Suite and Google connections	Fully integrating CRM and many other functions.	$30

Post Scheduling Systems

Product	URL	Functions	Notes	$/Mo
Buffer	www.buffer.com	Provides scheduling of posts to popular social media, including Twitter, Facebook, LinkedIn, Instagram, more.	Upgrade for more features	Free
Hootsuite	www.hootsuite.com	Provides scheduling of posts to popular social media, including Twitter, Facebook, LinkedIn, Instagram, more.	Upgrade for more features	Free
Tweetdeck	www.tweetdeck.twitter.com	Mange Twitter accounts, schedule posts, more.	Twitter only	Free

6

The Importance of Branding

How the cowboys got it right.

Way back in the 1880's most of the American West was a vast, unfenced area – rangeland punctuated by dramatic mountains and perilous arroyos. Cattle roamed freely and herds belonging to different ranchers often intermixed. Cowboys needed to tell which cattle belonged to whom on the open range.

Back then, establishing a brand meant marking all your cattle with a hot iron that permanently burned your mark into each animal's hide. Today, every brand manager longs to create a mark as permanent as that.

We're all familiar with many modern brands. The words coke, nike, apple, scotch, windows, and many others have had their historical meanings blurred by the simple addition of a capital letter. Now those are international brands, carrying deep and often complex emotional and intellectual meaning to millions, if not billions, of people.

This branding sword cuts both ways. Think of xerox, kleenex, post-it, margarine, and band-aid. These were, or are, trademarked brands. But through carelessness, these valuable properties have become common nouns – with a substantial loss of value for the companies that own them.

Virtually every successful organization has created a strong brand. This applies just as much to nonprofits as it does to for-profit enterprises. Think about what these brands mean to you, and how you respond emotionally to them:

- Red Cross
- YouTube
- Tea Party
- Girl Scouts
- IBM

- Salvation Army
- Apple
- Greenpeace
- Honda
- Google

See what I mean? Whether you love them or hate them, brands rule the mind-space of consumers world-wide.

Building your brand

Whether you are a marketer in the private sector or in the non-profit world, building and maintaining your brand is the most important work you have. A strong brand creates recognition of your organization and eliminates the need to explain its purpose. It creates trust (when properly maintained) and makes sales and support solicitations much easier. A good brand makes it easier to introduce new programs or products, and it helps to build a strong base of support. In fact, a strong brand makes every aspect of communications and marketing easier and more effective.

Building a strong brand takes imagination and hard work. But more than that, more important than a great logo or an unforgettable tag line is one thing: consistency. To build a great brand you must watch it like a zealous guard dog – shepherd it through difficult times, stand up for it if bullies attack, guard its reputation, and be sure it shows up at the right place, at the right time, and looking good. Here are few tips for building and maintaining a great brand.

Ensure appropriateness: If you're selling muscle cars, you don't want a pink floral logo. If you're a nonprofit pushing aid to the poor, a gold trimmed annual report is not appropriate. Bold ideas need bold representation; delicate subjects must be treated with discretion. Your logo needs to convey the key aspects of your organization at a glance. This is not a place to skimp. Pay a professional and get a great logo. It's worth every cent.

Be sure your logo works in every size, and in black and white: Your designer arrives to show you some logo concepts and they all look great. Each one is presented to you in beautiful color, about ten inches wide. But be sure to look at it one inch wide, as well. And look at it in black and white. You have to use your logo on stationary, advertising, signs, bags, pens, and websites. Be certain it works in every size and every potential location. Step across the room and see if it works from that distance.

Get a great tagline: The tagline is the short description that often accompanies your logo. Be sure it succinctly tells your story in as few words as possible. Try to make it catchy, even poetic. Great taglines take on a life of their own. Remember "It's the real thing?" How about "Breakfast of champions?" Your tagline augments the logo in building your identity in the minds of your constituents.

Use it everywhere: Don't be shy. Now that you have a great logo and tagline, be sure to use it everywhere you can. It's OK if it's small, or tucked in a corner. Be sure you use it in a consistent manner and with enough space around it that it stands out. Also be sure your constituents see it every chance they have. That's what creates name and identity recognition. And it takes more exposure than you may expect.

Messaging is part of your brand: The way your organization speaks and the exact words it uses to describe itself, its mission and its clients all help create your brand. Remember, your brand is in the mind of the beholder. Keep it clear and consistent so that it's easy to remember.

Be consistent: *Do not ever* change the shape or color of your logo. It will simply muddle perceptions and reduce recognition. During the design process, have your designer provide mockups of many likely usages to test how your logo works. Never change how you state your mission. Always keep your tag line exactly the same. This consistency may get boring to you, but it helps your image stick in the minds of your audience.

Use it long after you're tired of it: Think about the logos you recognize instantly, like Coke, IBM, or the Red Cross. They haven't changed in decades. Neither should yours. People don't like change, and when you change your identity people will wonder why. Stick with it. Consistent messaging pays marketing dividends.

Occasionally a new branding effort is in order. If your organization changes its direction or adds new programs, you may want to consider rebranding. Proceed with caution, because a well established brand is money in the bank and you do not want to waste it. A rebranding effort requires thoughtful attention to details, and must be rolled out with explanations that make sense and a transition plan that enables you to keep your old recognition while building your new image. It's complicated, and requires the utmost care. I have seen rebranding fail more often that succeed, because people don't realize how much recognition, and even love, their old brand has earned.

Don't dilute your brand: Sometimes organizations start new programs or launch new products, and try to use their existing brand for leverage. Sometimes this works, sometimes it doesn't. According to John Parham, president of Parham Santana, a brand extension consultancy, "A successful and lasting brand extension franchise must have three things: a logical fit with the parent brand; leverage for competitive advantage, and; opportunity to enhance the brand and produce sales."

Brand extension can add credibility to a new product. Consider DayQuil, an offshoot of the very popular NyQuil brand. This brand extension worked, probably because NyQuil had a strong brand and DayQuil is such a logical extension of it. But what about "Chicken Soup for the Pet Lovers Soul Pet Food," or "Dr. Pepper BBQ Sauce?" (Those are both real products!) A bad brand extension dilutes the impact of your primary brand, and can actually become a laughingstock. Beware!

Branding includes other components, including colors, overall look and feel, theme songs, mascots, and so on. Branding is the sum total of the impressions your customers and others have of your organization. As I said earlier, your brand is your organization's single greatest asset. Guard it like gold – for it is worth far more.

7

You May Have Heard This Before

The importance of consistent messaging

Like branding, of which messaging is part, how you talk about your organization and programs requires dedication and consistency. Consistent messaging is the heart of System Marketing.

Have you ever seen a TV commercial and thought, "Can't they think of anything else to say?" Have you ever found yourself with a jingle rattling around your brain, hours after you heard it on the radio? Have you glanced at an ad in a magazine, recognized the company, and turned the page without reading the ad? If you answered "yes" to any of these questions, you've been a target of effective and consistent messaging.

One of the prime characteristics of effective messaging is that it's boring. Boring that is, to those who create it, because it seldom changes. Boring, perhaps, to those who hear it, because they are constantly being told the same thing. But not boring at all to those who rely on people understanding their organization, because effective messaging creates an image in the mind of your customer that is long-lasting, cohesive, and easy to remember. Effective messaging requires repetition, long after you are tired of it. Be bored, it's OK.

Messaging includes every public representation of your organization. That includes your logo, your tagline, what the CEO says at the Rotary Club, how your receptionist answers the phone, the sales literature, your trade show presence – essentially, every public manifestation. As a marketer, your goal is to create a consistent and coherent message that hammers a few key points over and over – until your customers know them as well as you do.

Messaging isn't a slogan, though. It's much more than that. Messaging is the overall impact that everything you say and do has on your customer. If you use blue and gold on your logo, but your ads are red and black, you have muddled your messaging. If your website proclaims, "The only product you need to create better relationships with your customers", but your business card says, "Great CRM System", you have created a dissonant and less effective message.

The keys to effective nonprofit messaging
For nonprofits, consistent, effective messaging is critical. Every nonprofit has a *Mission Statement*. That's where your messaging starts, but not where it ends. Your organization also needs a *Needs Statement*, a *Vision Statement*, and a USP, or *Unique Selling Proposition*. Let me explain each one and how they differ.

Your needs statement is a quick explanation of why your organization exists and why people should support it. Your stakeholders need to believe that your organization is meeting a critical need, and doing it better than your competitors. Your messaging should describe a need that is relatively unchanging.

Your needs statement is the rationale behind your vision and mission. For example, it might read like this: "Thousands of children in Central America go to bed hungry every night. If their parents understood a few recent discoveries about farming in their region, they could produce 50% more maize and feed their children well every night."

Your *Vision* derives from the Need, and is what you hope to accomplish in the long term, such as, "ending hunger in Central America." Your *Mission Statement* describes how you fulfill your vision. You might say, "We will end hunger in Central America by teaching locals how to farm more effectively."

Like commercial enterprises, each nonprofit also needs to have a "Unique Selling Proposition (USP)." This is made up of a few key points that differentiate your organization from others with similar missions – your competition, as perceived by your customers.

Your customers will perceive competitors, so you need to offer a unique reason that they should support *your* organization instead of any other. There is a limited pot of donor money out there. Your unique selling proposition is key to differentiating your organization from all the others. In our example, the USP might be, "We provided more money to support farmer training than any other organization. Last year we helped 8,431 farmers learn new techniques so their children had enough to eat. Won't you help?"

Your your Needs, Vision, and Mission Statements and your USP

On competition

I have heard dozens of clients in for-profits and nonprofits tell me that they have no competition. That is bunkum.

Competition is not only who you think competes with you for donor dollars, quality people, or mindshare. Your true competition is who your customers think of instead of you. It's the name in your client's mind that you wish was yours. Your competition may not even seem to be in the same business as you, but your clients may perceive it differently. Your challenge is to stand out. That's where your strong messaging saves the day.

form the basis for all of your messaging. Be sure that everything flows from those key statements, and that every opportunity for communicating your message is clear, consistent, and true to those ideals.

Here are some key questions that will help you evaluate how consistent your messaging is:

- Do you present your Needs, Vision, and Mission Statements consistently?
- Have you identified and codified your Unique Selling Proposition?
- Does your logo look the same in every usage?
- Is your color scheme simple and consistent?
- How often does your tagline change?
- Is the look of your website and literature appropriate to your company, products, and customers?
- Are your customers comfortable with the language you use?
- Do you consistently make the same sales arguments (your USP)?
- Do you always describe your programs in the same way?
- Do your service or product names relate to each other and to the company name?

If your messaging is consistent, and true to your Needs, Vision, and Mission Statements, and USP, you will find that soon your customers are parroting it back to you, and even your competitors will start to talk about your organization in your terms. Everyone in the office will use the same terminology. That's good messaging.

8

Building Your Messaging Foundation

In which we go deeper into our organization's messaging

In this chapter I come back to messaging, addressing how you put together your message. Every service organization has a mission statement. Most have vision and needs statements as well. In this chapter we will look at developing those three statements, and we'll build a Case Statement from them.

In the previous chapter I talked about Mission, Vision, and Needs Statements. In terms of donor communications, they are the foundation. All of your communications must be based on these three statements. Your Systems Marketing plan requires that these statements be clear and concise.

I'm repeating some of this because it is so important and because I often see messaging done poorly.

Let's briefly reiterate: The *Needs Statement* is the first level of explanation. It demonstrates that your organization is meeting a critical need, and doing it better than anyone else. Your needs statement is the rationale behind the vision and mission. In our example, it might read like this: "Thousands of children in Central America go to bed hungry every night. If their parents were to use different seed and learn a few simple techniques, they could produce 50% more maize and feed their children enough every day."

Your *Vision Statement* should be brief and to the point. It might sound like, "By 2020, no Central American child goes to bed hungry."

Your *Mission Statement* describes what you do, how, and for whom. It too, should be short and sweet. Avoid building a single sentence mission statement that includes a bunch of dependent clauses and runs 150 words. Read it out loud. If you need to take a breath in the middle it's too long. You might say, "We will end hunger in Central America by teaching the indigenous peoples how to farm more effectively."

Building on emotion: the Case Statement

The Needs, Vision, and Mission statements build a logical case for people to support your organization. But logic is not enough. In fact, virtually no one buys (or donates) anything based on logic. People open their wallets when they open their hearts. So, how does your organization provide that essential tug to the heart-strings? By crafting a compelling Case Statement.

If you've ever stayed up watching late-night TV, you have probably seen ads for the Christian Children's Fund. I can't tell you if this is a good charity or not. But I can tell you that they have set the bar high for forging an emotional connection to their donors.

The Christian Children's Fund's TV spots typically start with a bearded, grizzled, world-weary man walking slowly though a third-world slum among ragged, possibly starving children who gaze at the passing camera with wide, sad eyes. He might be an off-duty reporter, or an explorer. He speaks directly to the camera and looks like he means what he says. This actor was chosen to do this ad for his deep voice, apparent sincerity and trustworthiness. He proceeds to describe the miserable lives these hungry, dirty, unschooled, apparently orphaned children endure. He paints a vivid picture of disease, hunger, abuse, poverty, and general despair. He brings tears to your eyes.

But wait! There is hope! If only you would send a small donation, barely enough to buy yourself a decent lunch, you can "adopt" one of these tykes, and save her from a life of horror. Now we see him holding a child, and her face is clean, and she's smiling. And you did it! Your tiny donation, that sum of money so paltry that you won't even notice it missing, has saved this poor child. Now, don't you feel better?

That's how you build an emotional case. The Case Statement is built on just three points, what I call the Key Three: the Need, the Solution, and the Ask.

1: **The Need:** There exists a terrible situation that needs to be fixed. Our hypothetical organization might explain it like this: "In the highlands of Central America, farms have become less productive over the past ten years. Soil is depleted and water is hard to come by. Changing climate in the area will probably make this dire situation worse. Children are already getting less to eat than they need to thrive, and infant mortality is high. Per capita income is less than $800 per year."

2: **The Solution:** We know how to fix it. Working with a team lead by Nobel Prize winner, Dr. Marie Curie, we have developed a new, natural hybrid of maize. It will grow in the increasingly warm and dry conditions we are seeing. As a bonus, this new breed of maize is more nutritious and insect resistant. Using this new seed, and some recently developed, simple techniques for managing their hill-side farms, the indigenous farmers in Central America will be able to grow more corn, feed their families better, and lift the standard of living of the entire region.

3: **The Ask:** With your help we will fix it. We can help the indigenous farmers of Central America remain in their centuries-old family homes. We can help their children get enough to eat, and because they are no longer hungry, a better education. We can help these proud people live longer, more productive, happier lives. All it takes is $329 to help an entire village – 200 people – live better lives. You can help an entire village, for less than a dollar a day — won't you pitch in?

Obviously, your Case Statement will be very different, but the three key points should be the heart of your messaging to donors. Once they are in place, it is vitally important that all of your messaging connects to them. I often suggest the development of an abridged version of these Key Three, which becomes a motto or slogan used on event invitations, your annual report, advertising, and brochures. This makes a pretty good elevator pitch, too. It can then be distilled down to a tagline, a shorter format yet.

For our example organization, our distilled case statement would come down to three sentences: There is a terrible problem for Central American indigenous people. Their farms are failing and people are hungry. Our organization has developed new seed and farming techniques that can solve the problem and let these people and their children lead longer, more productive lives.

As a tagline, the message would be boiled down even further, to its essence: Feeding the indigenous people of Central America by providing seeds and knowledge.

Spread the Word

As I said earlier, the most important aspect of coordinated and cohesive communications is System Marketing™. System Marketing builds on the fact that every communications function in your organization has a marketing impact, be it good or bad. That means that everyone in your organization, from the receptionist, to the executive director, to the President of the Board, needs to be aware of the impact of what they say and how they say it. The person who answers the phones (and PLEASE, don't use one of those awful automated response systems!) needs to be knowledgeable and friendly. Everyone in the organization needs to know the elevator pitch, and all of your communications need to be keyed to your needs, vision, and mission statements. That's the "system" in System Marketing – all communications, at all times, in every environment, by every member of the team, provides the same message.

For many nonprofits, development, or fund raising, is the primary outbound communications function. But it is seldom the only MarCom effort, and so all of your communications need to connect and strengthen each other. System Marketing, informed by strong Needs, Vision, Mission, and Case statements, will ensure that all of your communications are cohesive and consistent. It will ensure that all of your people understand the foundation of your communications, and as an added benefit, it will make it easier to do your job, since you will not have to rethink the basis of your communications whenever you create a new program or communications vehicle.

9

The 4 C's of Good Communications

More on Messaging

Talking is not communicating. Sending a million emails is not communicating. Yelling from atop a soapbox in the town square is not communicating. Printing a glamorous four-color brochure is not communicating. Sending out a well-written press release is not communicating. Buying time on radio is not communicating.

Communication requires a receptive audience. A message has to be heard and understood to be considered communication.

It seems obvious, doesn't it? Yet it is remarkable how many efforts to "communicate" fail to get their message across. I am constantly amazed by websites that fail to describe the service or product being sold until you dig through virtual reams of copy and pointless pictures. Or how many nonprofit people falter when it comes to explaining their mission, vision, and programs in language that lay people can understand.

There are several issues that cause these problems. As a follow up to the last chapter on messaging, let me go a little deeper.

In the previous chapter I talked about the importance of consistent messaging. The crux of consistent messaging is that all of your materials, and all of your people, need to be on the same wavelength and providing a consistent message to all comers. That's the system in System Marketing. The other side of that coin is what your messaging says. In other words, you can be very consistent, but be saying the wrong things. Saying the right things can make a really big difference in the success of your organizations.

The 4 Cs

Your communications need to be **Consistent, Clear, Concise,** and **Contextual**. I discussed the first C, "consistent," in the last chapter. Now let's go through the other three C's of messaging.

Clear: Is there anything that is not clear about your messaging? You should be able to describe your organization's work so that someone who has no knowledge of your group can quickly grasp what you do. Use simple language and words that are easy to understand. People will not work to get your message, so keep it simple and easy to comprehend. Clear messages look like this:

- Earthjustice is a nonprofit public interest law firm dedicated to protecting the magnificent places, natural resources, and wildlife of this earth and to defending the right of all people to a healthy environment.

- Since its founding in 1881 by visionary leader Clara Barton, the American Red Cross has been the nation's premier emergency response organization.

- TechSoup Stock connects nonprofits and public libraries with donated and discounted technology products.

- GuideStar's mission is to revolutionize philanthropy and nonprofit practice by providing information that advances transparency, enables users to make better decisions, and encourages charitable giving.

- Springboard Schools is a nonprofit network of educators committed to raising student achievement and narrowing the achievement gap.

Concise: Remember, even your long-form description of the organization should be no more than 100 words, and (Now, this is important!) each sentence should be no more than about ten words. People forget the beginning of your sentence if you haven't finished it within about ten words. Many nonprofits, especially academically-oriented groups, have a problem with this. One organization I used to work with seemed to need to impress people with their vocabulary. I describe their method of communication as never using 10 words when 100 would do. Don't fall into that trap! Nobody cares how many words you know. They care about understanding what you do.

A good elevator pitch is essential to successful communication with donors and program participants. This short-form presentation is based on the idea that you are in an elevator and need to describe your organization before your fellow rider departs. You have 30 seconds. What will you say?

The clear messages I noted above are also great elevator pitches. Take another look at them, and then practice getting your descriptive message down to 15-30 seconds. Remember: use short, punchy sentences and unambiguous language. Practice saying it out loud and work on it until your eleavtor pitch flows smoothly and naturally and tells your story.

Contextual: This means that your message fits your audience, mission, and vision. Keeping your message contextual means not getting sidetracked. For example, if your organization provides seminars on gender equality for HR professionals, you should not start off by talking about the technology that enables your online discussions. A contextual message stays on topic and is not cluttered with interesting but nonessential information. Remember, data and information are not the same. Supply just the data needed to back up your information, not a lot of extraneous facts or opinions.

Contextual messages also relate to whom and when you are communicating. If you are talking to your U.S. Senator, you want to address concerns that relate to national policy; how your organization can help, and what you need to get the job done. Your Mayor will be more interested in local aspects of your program, such as how many people in your city are being helped. If you are talking to high-value donors, you'll want to stress the big picture, the great need, the wonderful work you do, and how their support of your organization will benefit them. If you are promoting an event, stress the value of attending, the reasonable cost, and the important contacts to be made there. Get the picture? Context is everything in communications.

To sum up: Your communications are how people know who you are and what you do. Remember the 4 C's of communications – **Consistent, Clear, Concise,** and **Contextual** – to ensure that your communications do the job for you and your organization.

10

The Marketing Mix

In which we become the DJ of our own exciting MarCom Hit Parade.

Today must be the best day ever to be a marketer. And tomorrow will be even better. Why? Because at no time in history have there been as many tools at our disposal, so many ways to reach our audiences, and so many ways to measure our effectiveness.

The key to successful marketing is using the appropriate media to reach your audience. The buzz these days is about using social media and the internet for marketing. Apparently no one ever recommended a product or service before the internet enabled that process! If you believe the hype, no one communicated before email, and the only advertising that matters are banners on web pages and text ads on Google. But I've been around awhile, so let me assure you that traditional technologies – paper, face-to-face communications, and the postal system are still effective ways to get your message to people. And when you combine modern electronic communications with those older, proven technologies, you can build strong and effective campaigns that meet your objectives and fit your budget. That combination of tools and techniques is called your Marketing Mix.

For those of us working in nonprofit MarCom, it is essential not to waste any of our typically too-small marketing budgets. I take pride in getting the most from every MarCom dollar by creating an effective marketing mix for every project. Sometimes you need print advertising, and sometimes you augment it with online ads. Usually you email press releases to journalists, but sometimes you need the in-hand impact of the printed sheet to cut through the noise and make an impression. In this age of constant email, I have found that an old-fashioned brochure in the mail can really get people's attention. But adding some well-placed advertising, and perhaps a press release announcing the event or program you are sponsoring can create a powerful marketing mix that gets better results.

Working in nonprofit MarCom, I have found that there are a few constraints that one seldom deals with in the business world. In high-tech marketing, it is hard to be too brash, to make a sales pitch that is too strong, or to be too flashy. In the social service world, people expect you to be a bit more modest, to not conspicuously spend money on marketing, and to be less blatantly competitive. Cultural issues also abound, and a diverse audience's sensibilities must be considered. And of course, one must not upset your donors. How you construct your message and what tools comprise your marketing mix are dependent on being sensitive to these issues, as well as to getting the response you need.

In the next few pages, I list the most common tools available to the NP MarCom team, give you some examples of what they are good for, evaluate their strengths and weaknesses, talk about their cost versus other methods, and give you some ideas about measuring effectiveness.

Remember that in many, if not most cases, you will be combining several of these tools to achieve the best result. Also, keep in mind that few organizations use all of these tools – it's important to determine which ones best meet your objectives and fit your budget. This list is by no means exhaustive, and the best MarCom minds are always thinking up new ways to communicate. So take this list as a starting point and let your imagination run free as you create your own marketing mix.

MarCom Tool, Advertising: Web/SEM

Good For
Branding
Selling products or services
Positioning vs. competitors
Event marketing
Backup to direct response
Reaching previously unknown people

Pros & Cons
Easy to access
Perishable – leave the site and the ad is gone
Hard to choose environment
Short lead time: easy to change quickly
Planning is key to effectiveness (being in the right place at the right time)

Relative Cost
Possibly lower cost for creative (than print)
Pay per click (PPC) reduces costs
Generally lower CPM (Cost Per Thousand impressions) than print
Testing is inexpensive

Impact
Instant response possible
Mind share
Product sales
Awareness of other media (read our book, follow us on Twitter)
Can be seen anytime, anywhere

ROI Metrics
Website visits
Email inquiries
Downloads
Phone calls
Product sales
Tradeshow attendance
Mindshare metrics (do people remember your message?)
Buzz

Good For Branding
Selling products or services
Connection to popular programs or causes
Positioning vs. competitors
Event marketing
Backup to direct response

Pros & Cons Easy to access
Perishable – leave the channel and the ad is gone
Makes advertiser look successful (if creative is good)
Can place ads in programs that relate to and reinforce your message
Short lead time: easy to change quickly
Planning is key to effectiveness (being in the right place at the right time)
Requires sophisticated buyer

Relative Cost Most expensive: creative and placement
Testing is expensive
Even minor changes can cost a lot

Impact Can reach large audiences
Repetition is good
Instant response possible
Mind share
Product sales
Awareness of other media

ROI Metrics Ratings supplied by third parties
Phone calls
Website visits
Downloads
Email inquiries
Product sales
Tradeshow attendance
Mindshare metrics

Good For Branding
Selling products or services
Positioning vs. competitors
Event marketing
Backup to direct response

Pros & Cons Requires long-term investment
Easy to access
Possible to choose placement
Staying power
Long lead time
Planning is key to effectiveness (being in the right place at the right time)

Relative Cost High: creative plus placement
Testing can be very expensive
Extra cost for premium placement
Long-term contracts reduce cost per ad

Impact Mind share
Product sales
Awareness of other media (visit our website, follow us on Facebook)

ROI Metrics Phone calls
Website visits
Email inquiries
Downloads
Product sales
Tradeshow attendance
Mindshare metrics

Good For Branding
Getting attention
Samples
Opening conversation at shows
Announcing special events

Pros & Cons Medium lead time
Hard to test
Often discarded quickly
Must be relevant
May be seen as tacky
Can create a lasting impression (good or bad)

Relative Cost Moderate, depending on items
Usually one of the lowest priorities in my budgets

Impact Usually modest
Easy to make a bad impression on many fronts
Can be effective in the right places

ROI Metrics Very difficult to measure as part of mix
Use as entrance ticket or for door prize entry

MarCom Tool, Promotion: Conferences, Conventions, and Trade Shows

Good For
Branding
Opening new territories
New product introduction
Distributing samples
Opportunity to meet customers face to face
Surveys
Selling products or services
Positioning vs. competitors
Competitive intelligence

Pros & Cons
Long lead time
Good planning is essential: strategy, staff training, booth design, handouts, follow up
Meet a lot of people in short time
Can coincide with other meetings and visits
Opportunities to speak are very valuable

Relative Cost
Can be very expensive:
Booth design
Literature
Handouts
Travel costs
Lost office time

Impact
Can reach large audiences
Deals made at shows
Instant response possible
Mind share
Product sales
Comparison to competitors

ROI Metrics
Leads collected
Sales made
Meetings scheduled
Website visits
Handouts distributed
Sales
Competitive knowledge gained
Met with right people
Deals made
Verbal and other feedback

Good For Branding
Opening new territories
New product introduction
Opportunity to meet customers face to face
News creation
Recognition of customers and donors
Raising money
Reaching policymakers

Pros & Cons Long lead time
Good planning is essential: strategy, staff training, venue, catering, decorating, event design, handouts, follow up
Meet a lot of people in short time
Can be very strong for PR and branding
If poorly run, can be PR disaster

Relative Cost Moderate to very expensive
May be offset by money raised

Impact Good vibes – everyone loves a party
Can attract donors
Can create loyalty, especially among award winners
Increases interest
Reinforces messaging
May create synergies among those who meet at event
Gets message to right people

ROI Metrics Donations
Press coverage
The right people attended
Verbal and other feedback
Website visits
Email inquiries
Phone calls
Mindshare metrics
Policy influenced
Mentions by policymakers

MarCom Tool, Promotion: Pens, T-shirts, cups, bags, magnets, desk accessories, etc., etc.

Good For
Branding
Repeated exposure of logo and message
Creating gratitude
"Free" advertising
Small reward to frequent customers
Memento of events

Pros & Cons
Quick and easy
If low quality, may reflect on badly on giver
Often simply thrown away, but
Can create lasting message
Good quality creates good impression
Can become valued souvenir

Relative Cost
Depends on item -- Can be surprisingly expensive
ROI can be high
Be sure gift is appropriate to recipient: Don't give a 39 cent pen to a million dollar donor.

Impact
Varies widely: can be very high
Helps create loyalty
Increases interest
Reinforces messaging
Gets message to right people

ROI Metrics
Requests for more
Obvious use of gift item
Seen on TV, Facebook, Twitter, etc.
Staff wants one
Other mentions

Good For Branding
Raising awareness among media
Providing long-form info
Providing multimedia (on disk or flash drive)
Establishing expertise

Pros & Cons Essential part of every media mix
Important for journalists
Can be used with donors
Must be high-quality and highly relevant to get attention
Electronic media kits very popular, allow inclusion of audio and video

Relative Cost Low

Impact Deferred: helps journalists know your program, mission, people
Increases interest
Reinforces messaging
Gets message to right people
Increased use of your facts, materials, knowledge

ROI Metrics Media contacts
Requests for more info
Requests for comments
Website visits
Attendance at press conferences
Downloads
Stories in media

Good For
Branding
Event marketing
Connecting to outside events
Maintaining awareness
Opening new territories
New product introduction
Staff announcements
Creating news
Supporting advertising
Establishing expertise
Strengthening relationships
Recognition

Pros & Cons
Best way to get "free" publicity
News reports have high credibility
Can establish expertise
Important backup to other efforts
If overdone, can be negative
Making a big deal out of nothing is seen negatively by journalists

Relative Cost
Low

Impact
Increased event attendance
Improved morale
Perception of expertise
Awareness of organization, program, mission, good deeds, etc.
Increased donations
Your story on TV or in other media

ROI Metrics
Value of print space
Number of mentions
Follow up by media
Phone calls
Website visits
Email inquiries
Product sales
Event attendance
Tradeshow attendance
Mindshare metrics

MarCom Tool, Public Relations: News Conference and Briefings

Good For
- Branding
- Media mindshare
- Connecting to outside events
- Exposure of top people
- Opening new territories
- New product introduction
- Hearing media questions
- Supporting advertising
- Establishing expertise
- Strengthening relationships
- Recognizing achievements
- Reaching policymakers

Pros & Cons
- Can provide much more info than a release alone
- Good way to present research findings
- Good for important announcements
- Opportunity to get materials in hands of journalists
- If poorly attended, can look bad
- Timing can be difficult: an unexpected big story can divert interest
- Establishing media relationships
- Face-to-face meeting with journalists

Relative Cost
- Moderate, depending on venue, refreshments, materials, audio/visual (A/V) requirements, travel, etc.

Impact
- Increased news coverage
- Perception of expertise
- Awareness of organization, people, program, mission, good deeds, etc.
- Relationships with journalists
- Policy influence
- Improved morale

ROI Metrics
- Attendance
- Value of printed space
- Number of mentions
- Follow up by media
- Phone calls
- Website visits
- Email inquiries
- Product sales
- Conference attendance
- Mindshare metrics
- Requests for more info
- Requests for comments
- Downloads

Good For Recognizing achievements and contributions
Reason for a party
Reason for press release
Exposure of top people
Branding
Opening new territories
Establishing expertise
Strengthening relationships
Reaching policymakers

Pros & Cons Creates lots of good will
Award selection process must be transparent and fair
Provides great PR opportunities
Creates allies
Can create animosities if not handled well.

Relative Cost Moderate, but awards can be expensive

Impact Increased news coverage
Perception of expertise
Increased awareness of organization, people, program, mission, good deeds, etc.
Policy influence
Improved morale
Strong allies

ROI Metrics Verbal and other feedback
Website visits
Email inquiries
Phone calls
Mindshare metrics
Policy influenced
Mentions by policymakers

Good For	Branding
	Meeting regulatory requirements
	Program promotion
	Establishing expertise
	Strengthening relationships
	Recognizing achievements
	Reaching policymakers
	Impressing donors
	Introduction to organization
Pros & Cons	Requested by some funders
	Often perceived as boring
	Can take a lot of time
	Must balance impact and flashiness
	Long lead time
	Can have very strong, positive impact
	Can demonstrate competence
Relative Cost	Varies widely
	Staff time requirement can be significant
Impact	Perception of expertise
	Awareness of organization, people, program, mission, good deeds, etc.
	Policy influence
	Improved morale
	Awareness among donors
ROI Metrics	Strengthened relationships
	Donations
	Verbal and other feedback
	Website visits
	Email inquiries
	Phone calls
	Mindshare metrics
	Mentions by policymakers

Good For   Branding
Program promotion
Establishing expertise
Reaching policymakers
Providing research results
Impressing donors
Introduction to organization
Publishing long-form information

Pros & Cons   Excellent way to provide detailed information
Good way to publish research
Fewer people are readers
Difficult to update
Long lead time

Relative Cost   Varies Widely
Publishing can be expensive.
Shipping paper is expensive
Staff time requirement can be significant

Impact   Reaches academics
Place in libraries
Shows expertise
Influences other experts
Long lasting reference
Increased donations
Income from book sales

ROI Metrics   Sales of book
Reviews
Amazon ranking
Donations
Verbal and other feedback
Website visits
Email inquiries
Phone calls
Mindshare metrics
Number of mentions
Follow up by media
Requests for comment
Citations
Policy influenced
Mentions by policymakers

Good For Branding
Providing stakeholders with inside info
Program promotion
Establishing expertise
Recognizing achievements
Reaching policymakers
Impressing donors
Introduction to organization

Pros & Cons Helps strengthen brand
Enables stakeholders to feel like insiders
Can occupy a lot of staff time.
Content may be difficult to get.
Requires strong writing skills
Requires strong design and layout skills

Relative Cost Moderate to high
Paper costs a lot more than an electronic edition
Can be distributed in a variety of ways, at varying
costs

Impact Provides current news
Promotes brand and products
Shows expertise
Influences other experts
Long lasting reference
Increased donations
Available 24/7
Portable

ROI Metrics Subscriptions
Response to content
Donations
Verbal and other feedback
Website visits
Email inquiries
Phone calls
Mindshare metrics
Sales
Event registrations

MarCom Tool, Publications: Website

Good For
Everything – the uber-media
Branding
Community building
News promulgation
Product info
Sales
Event promotion
Recognizing achievements
Reaching policymakers
Soliciting donors
Providing information in any format
Soliciting feedback

Pros & Cons
Intense competition for attention
A poor site will turn off visitors
Easily updated
Short lead times
Presents a variety of media
Invites participation at many levels

Relative Cost
Moderate to high
Internal management greatly reduces cost
Frequent updates add to maintenance cost

Impact
Instant response possible
Mind share
Product sales
Can reach large audiences
Available 24/7, worldwide

ROI Metrics
Donations
Verbal and other feedback
Sales
Event participation
Website visits
Downloads
Email inquiries
Phone calls
Mindshare metrics
Mentions by policymakers
Time on site
Pages visited

Good For
Increasing effectiveness of website
Building community
Soliciting feedback
Encouraging participation
Soliciting content
Viral marketing

Pros & Cons
Can be gimmicky
Great way to build community
Great feedback mechanism
Encourages free content creation
Very difficult to trigger virality

Relative Cost
Moderate to set up, low to maintain

Impact
Community building
Instant response possible
Mind share
Product sales
Can reach large audiences
Available 24/7, worldwide
Perceived as "with it"

ROI Metrics
Participation
Friend
Followers
Cross links (retweets, etc.)
Buzz
Donations
Verbal and other feedback
Sales
Event participation
Website visits
Downloads
Email inquiries
Mindshare metrics

Good For
Sales
Event registration
Donor solicitation
Surveys
New product information
Expanding area of influence
Coupons

Pros & Cons
Increasingly effective as way to avoid avalanche of email
Slow delivery
Easy to measure response
Easy to test
Good creative essential
One mailer can contain several types of material

Relative Cost
Varies widely

Impact
Mind share
Product sales
Can reach large audiences
Available 24/7

ROI Metrics
Response is directly measurable
Website visits
Phone calls
Email
Sales
Inquiries

Good For Sales
Event registration
Donor solicitation
Surveys
New product information
Expanding area of influence
Coupons

Pros & Cons Immediate delivery
Short lead time
Easy to measure response
Easy to test
Good creative essential
Can include a variety of electronic media
Can contain web links
May get lost in spam filters
Can turn off recipients

Relative Cost Low

Impact Mind share
Product sales
Can reach large audiences
Available 24/7

ROI Metrics Response is directly measurable
Website visits
Phone calls
Email
Sales
Inquiries

Good For Providing targets for direct response
Evaluating other efforts
Isolating people with similar demographics,
locations, or interests
Getting messages to carefully targeted sub-groups of
your mailing list

Pros & Cons Requires good database
Requires conscientious maintenance and data entry
Provides unique ability to segregate and aggregate
constituents

Relative Cost Moderate to high
Setup costs can be very high
Staff involvement is high
Errors may be difficult to fix

Impact Better targeting of messages
Cost savings from bad addressing
Income enhancement from more efficient marketing
Adds value to lists you already have (or should have)

ROI Metrics Provides tools to measure all other efforts
Improvements in response
Reduced returned and bounced mail

11

Marketing vs. Sales

Marketing and sales go together like a teenager and SnapChat. But they are substantially different, and most organizations need both.

Among many people in the nonprofit world, sales has a bad reputation. At one nonprofit, which included in its mission providing consulting services to public organizations, I had a senior manager tell me directly, "We don't do sales." (That organization is now on a downward spiral.) Now, in your work in a nonprofit, you may also be thinking, "We don't do sales." But my friend, you are wrong.

- If you have a development team working to raise money for your organization, they are doing sales.

- If you have a program for which you recruit qualified people, you are doing sales.

- If you have a book or report that you are trying to get people to read – even for free – you are doing sales.

- If you have an event for which you are trying to fill seats, you are doing sales.

- If you are recruiting people to sit on your board of directors, yes, you are doing sales.

Get the picture? Selling is almost precisely equivalent to persuasion. You don't have to ask for money to make a sale. (Remember when you "sold" your mate on the vacation you really wanted?) Sales occur when someone is providing value to you or your organization at your bequest. That value can be a donation, the most obvious "sale," or it can be volunteering to help, arranging an introduction, or sending someone to meet with the Executive Director. When you are persuading people to work with your organization, support it, or make use of its programs, you are making a sale. "Sales" is not a dirty word. Everything you wear, everything you eat, everything you drive, virtually everything that surrounds you, was once sold.

Don't be bothered that your organization has to make sales. Just be ethical and honest and the rest is easy to handle.

So, back to the initial question,: What is the difference between marketing and sales? The terms are often confused, but there are important and substantial differences.

Let me define what each of these essential activities is.

Marketing is:

- The inside part of the sales process
- The preparation to make a sale
- The communication function that drives sales
- The research that helps an organization know what to sell
- Deciding where, when, and whom to approach regarding your services and products
- The backup information needed to make a sale
- Working with a journalist on a story about your

organization

- Publishing a newsletter
- Building a great website
- Advertising to gain support
- Analyzing sales results
- Creating a great annual report
- Publicizing events

On the other hand, sales is:

- The outside part of the sales process
- Discussing a product or service face to face
- Structuring a deal
- Asking for business or support
- Negotiating the details of a transaction
- Asking a policymaker for help, or to support a position
- Following up with customers
- Looking for new customers

Like a horse and carriage, sales won't go far without marketing. And likewise, marketing without sales is usually ineffective. In a nonprofit, the MarCom efforts provide a foundation for development work, program outreach, event management, and many other functions. While you may not think that convincing a policymaker to read your white paper is a sales function, I assure you that having a strong MarCom effort that has previously acquainted that policymaker with your organization will make your task much easier.

So remember. Those of us who work in the social services sector are in sales. And we need a strong MarCom function to make our work more effective.

12

Websites 101: Making Your Website Findable

SEO is not a beach in Brazil

I've got a website. You've got a website. Everybody 'cept Granny has a website. (And hers is under construction.)

But have you ever asked, why?

We all know that our website is important. But do we know how to make it really work for us?

SEO stands for Search Engine Optimization. It refers to techniques that make it easier for search engines, such as Google, Bing, and Yahoo, to find your website and index its contents. SEO is the little extra that helps our website really deliver.

There are a lot of good reasons to have an organizational website. It has become a requirement of a legitimate business, replacing the once-ubiquitous yellow pages ad with a colorful, ever-changing multimedia extravaganza. That's the website bottom line: We exist.

But that's a low bar. There are many more reasons to have a website, and a good website can be a tremendous booster for your organization. I'll cover the basics quickly, then talk about a few advanced techniques that can really improve the ROI on your website. There are two key factors related to a successful website: getting people to it, and keeping them there. In this chapter I'm talking about how to get people to your website. In the next I'll talk about keeping them there, what is called the "stickiness" of the site.

Like the lead of a news story, your website needs to include the Five W's – or links to them. If you ever took a journalism class, you recall that the five W's are:

- **Who:** Who we are, "Allied Rooster Breeders of Tulsa"

- **What:** What we do, "We assure the purity of rooster bloodlines by maintaining accurate breeding records. We also produce events that enable the rooster breeding community to meet, do business, and socialize."

- **Why:** The reason we exist, "Rooster breeders have long needed a voice and a standards board."

- **When:** Not always appropriate, but this could mean, "Since 1841", or "We protect rooster breeders 24 hours a day." Your call.

- **Where:** Where are you located and where do you work, "Contact us at this address, email, or phone number," or, "We serve rooster breeders in the Tulsa River Valley area."

Hitting each of the five W's on your home page will enable visitors to know immediately where they are and why. Then they will need to know how to find the information they came for, using what is called the Site Navigation, another key website element. Your site navigation includes:

- The buttons and links that take visitors to various items and pages. These should be easy to read, and ideally, should provide audio or visual feedback when used.

- A menu that is obvious and takes people where they want to go as quickly as possible. Don't get too cute with the menu. Especially as the population of over-40's increases, you need a menu that is easy to find and read, and not challenging to use.

- The site navigation is based on a logical and shallow hierarchy of information and pages, so that it is quickly apparent how to find things. Try to make your site organization shallow – more wide than deep. By that, I mean that you don't want to build a site that forces users to click after click after click after click after click to find what they wants. Many rich sites are only three or four clicks deep. To build a shallow site, make your second levels large and scalable. For example, you may have only two programs now, but your programs page could have room for ten.

- Have a site search function. Google offers a free site search widget, as do several other companies. You can customize the look of the Google widget and limit search to your site, or the entire internet. Having a search function makes it really easy for visitors to find a name, date, place, or other bit of information that could take hours to find any other way. Having a search box is just being a good neighbor.

- Finally, site navigations should always include a site map, detailed to at least the second level of your site. I believe that a site map should provide a primary navigation for visitors who want to go directly to a bit of information. A site map to the third level will cover a lot of pages, and enable quick navigation.

Back to "Why"

Once you build a website with all of the five W's and good navigation — your basic internet version of a yellow pages ad — you may have looked at it and thought, "We still have infinite room. How do we fill it?" This is when the "Why?" question must be faced.

Ideally, you addressed "why" before you started. But it is better to have your internet shingle hung out than not to exist in cyberspace. Let's talk about "why" now.

By *why*, I mean, what do you want your website to do for the organization? We have established the basic function: we exist. Now you can use your website to fulfill a number of additional objectives. Here are some of the most frequently seen:

- Most organizations have a lot of information they are trying to get out to people – their sites have a library function.

- We all have seen online shopping sites. Many organizations sell books and other merchandise using an online store.

- Nonprofits typically rely on donations. Those organizations have a donation processing system built into their website.

- If an organization produces events, or provides classes, it would benefit from an online registrations system.

- And by the way, you'll need a calendar of those events. Integration with common downloadable and online calendars is a nice bonus.

People flock to nonprofits for the communities that form around them. Make it easy for your community to meet and talk by including web features like a video upload section (connected to YouTube or Vimeo), blogs, text message delivery, podcasts, recorded webinars, and other items your community will find useful.

People have questions and suggestions. To give them quick answers, provide a FAQ, a page of Frequently Asked Questions, and their answers. To help visitors find people, add a complete list of staff and provide email links and/or phone numbers. Also provide a contact/feedback form that makes it easy for visitors to get in touch with you with questions or suggestions.

Most importantly, most organizations have a program of activities in which visitor can participate. A detailed explanation of what your programs comprise, including when and where they occur, who they are best suited for, what they cost and why people should attend. (There's those five W's again.)

What should the home page of your website include? What should it look like? Those are among the most asked questions whenever I help people work on their websites. Everybody has an idea, everybody wants to put the most important programs front and center. What makes this a real conundrum is that there is seldom an easy answer to this question.

There are crowded home pages, like Craig's List and Idealist.org, that have every inch covered with text or pictures. Those are portals: like an airport, once you enter the gate you have many destination options. Other sites make more use of white space, and direct your eyes to a few, very important words or images. Google's home page is an extreme example of this.

There is no absolute rule for deciding how much goes on your home page except to say what you need to say, and nothing more.

There are also no absolute rules on what your website should look like. In my opinion, the current state of maturity in website design borders on boring. With the wide acceptance of Word Press, too many sites look alike. This isn't all bad – Word Press is relatively easy to use and lowers development costs. But I believe that a distinct website design can strengthen your branding and help your organization stand out from the crowd. I recommend investing in a custom design if you can possibly afford it.

Your website design should be easy to comprehend, easy to read, and relate to your mission. The design should never detract from your message and should keep your community and constituencies in mind. Skip the 9 point, light grey type – boomers won't make the effort to read it. But, if your audience is young and edgy your website should reflect that in its design. Remember that your website usually will have several different audiences. Your donors need different information than your clients. Your staff may need a section for itself. And perhaps the general public will be checking in to see what you are doing. Design to have something that will reach each audience segment without offending the others.

Your website also needs to be responsive. This is a technical term that means it automatically adjusts to fit whatever screen it is being viewed on. A responsive website looks good on a mobile phone, a tablet, or a large monitor. Responsiveness is essential in modern website design.

On being seen

So you've had a beautiful website built, everyone agrees that it is a work of art and easy to use. Now, how do you get people to see it?

I have been surprised several times by people who launch their first website and then a week after, ask me why they are not getting many visitors. Well, it goes like this. When a website is first published, it can take several weeks for the search engines to find it. It can then take days more before the site is listed in search results. And unless you have a very prominent site, it will be way down in those results. So, the likelihood of a new site being found immediately by lots of people is very low.

But all is not lost. There are several techniques to improve search engine ranking (how near the top you are) and to use search engines to draw visitors to your site. The first is called Search Engine

Optimization (SEO), and the second is Search Engine Marketing (SEM). Both are key to successful internet marketing. I'll talk about SEO in this chapter, and address SEM in the next.

SEO is intended to make it easy for the search engines to find your site and recognize its content. There are several factors that can make or break your site in regard to search engines:

- Don't get too flashy. *Flash* is a technology that allows a great amount of freedom for web designers. It makes really nice, fancy transitions, like fading pictures with sound effects, and makes it possible to display animations and video. But Flash has a big drawback. The content of a Flash animation cannot be read by search engines. Sites that rely heavily on Flash must go to extraordinary lengths to be indexed properly for search. If you use Flash go easy, and be sure to use the other tools I talk about here.

- Use meta tags: Meta tags are information your web pages include that helps them be displayed properly and to be found and indexed for searching. There are three key meta tags every site should use. They are:

  - Title: The title appears on the top of the browser window when your pages are displayed. It should say something meaningful. "Welcome to our home page" is NOT meaningful. A good title will describe the page contents very briefly, and include your organization's name. A good title might be, "Why Roosters Are Important — Allied Rooster Breeders of Tulsa," or "Meet the Board of Directors — Allied Rooster Breeders of Tulsa."

  - Description: This meta tag contains just what it says, a brief description of your site. This will appear when people bookmark your website, and is used by search engines to help categorize your site. Take some time to write a good, short description, and then add it to every page of your site. If you like, each page can have a unique description.

- Keywords: Keywords are the simple words and phrases that describe your site. Think of how you would search for your site on Google or Yahoo. Those words should be your keywords. While some search engines are moving away from a reliance on keywords, many still use them. I like to have a basic set of keywords that are used on every page, along with a group for each page that focuses on that page's content.

- Cross links: These are links to your site from other sites. Work with your partners to mutually link to each other's sites. This will help build traffic for all of the organizations.

- Create a machine-readable, XML sitemap: A machine-readable site map is an XML file placed in the root directory as your website. Now that sounds a bit technical, and it is, but your webmaster will understand how to build and where to put your XML site map. There are a number of sites on the internet that will create free XML sitemaps for you. These are used by search engines to understand the structure and content of your site. They are not easily read by people because they are machine to machine communication. One of my favorite sites is www.xml-sitemaps.com.

- Remember those five W's we talked about earlier: Be sure that each of them is on your home page. They don't have to be large or prominent – you might have your contact information in a very small font at the bottom of the page. But search engines read your pages and build their indices based on what they read. It is absolutely essential that you home page contain enough information that the search engine knows what it is reading and what it means. And by the way, your visitors will find your site more easily, and when they get there, they will find it more useful.

- Use a submission service: Submission services automate the process of informing many search engines that your website exists or has changed significantly. I use them when things have changed dramatically, and when I launch a new site. I also use them every year or so to help keep my listings fresh. I have never spent more than $50 for a submission service, and don't recommend that you do either. These services send your site information to a dozen or more search engines. So, while Google, Microsoft, Yahoo, and AOL have about 90% of the search market, a submission services will get you them, plus another 7-8%. It's not worth a lot, but it is worth something.

That's it for Search Engine Optimization. Using these techniques I have increased website traffic dramatically. You can do the same. In the next chapter, I'll talk about Search Engine Marketing, the flip side of adding value to your website, and website stickiness, the science of keeping people on your site longer.

13

Making Search Engines Work For You

The ABC's of SEM

We use search engines to find all kinds of stuff on the World Wide Web. Search for restaurants, search for clothes, search for old boy-

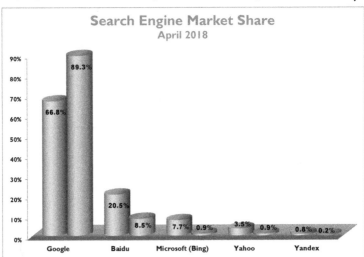

This chart makes it obvious why people "google" their questions. Nearly 70% market share (almost 90% on mobile devices) makes Google the 600 pound gorilla. Blue is desktop search, green is mobile devices.

friends, search for a place to get parts for that 1957 Lionel steam locomotive. You can search for recipes, songs, and even nonprofits that deserve your support.

According to the College of Marketing website (http://www.collegeofmarketing.com/seo-guide/search-engine-usage/), there are more than 100 billion global searches done every month. These numbers are increasing daily. The chart above shows the market share of the most popular search engines as of April, 2018.

As nonprofit marketers, the questions we need to ask include; how do we get good ranking in search engines, and how do we ensure that our site shows up when someone searches for a related topic?

We talked about search engine optimization (SEO) in the last chapter. SEO techniques ensure that our site is properly seen and indexed by the search engine programs that wander around the web and look for changes. (These programs are called crawlers or spiders.) SEO enable us to feel confident that our site will show up in searches where our stakeholders are likely to find it. The next step is to find ways that we can use the search engines as marketing tools, to improve event attendance, increase donations, add new members, get more attention, or sell products.

In addition to SEO, there are two legitimate ways to be included in search engine results: *Paid Inclusion* and *Paid Advertising*, also known as *Pay Per Click (PPC)*.

Paid Inclusion

Paid inclusion is simple. It means you pay the search engine to accelerate its indexing of your website.

There are many internet entrepreneurs offering a variety of submission services, with varying promises and prices ranging from nothing to several hundred, or even thousands, of dollars. As I mentioned in the SEO chapter, I use these services sparingly, and refuse to pay large amounts for their sometimes dubious services.

Another way to get on to search engine result pages is banner advertising. I'm going to talk about advertising in general later, but keep in mind that paying for an ad on a results page can give you very high page rank, at a price. Only a few general-purpose search engines accept banner ads, but many special interest and news sites are happy to have them.

Paid Advertising

Paid, or Pay Per Click (PPC), advertising is chosen to appear on a page because it is relevant to the search being conducted. For example, if I search for "hunting boots" I may see ads for a hunting lodge, a shoe store, an outdoor supply company, a boot manufacturer, and a gun shop. You get the picture. The ads are often sold in a type of auction. I'm most familiar with Google's AdWords program, so that's what I'll use for examples.

A major concern in search engine advertising is where on the page your message appears. Page ranking refers to how high on the page your message or website appears. Obviously, being listed first in a search result is best. Being the first ad on the page is also good. Keep in mind that you want your message to appear on the screen of the searcher, no matter what screen resolution (which controls how much information is displayed at once). I call this "above the fold," a phrase which was borrowed from the newspaper industry. What's above the fold on your newspaper's front page is what you see first – that's where the lead stories are. You always want your message above the fold. You can't buy placement in the search results on the major engines, so instead, you buy advertising.

When you buy ads to run on Google, after establishing an account and a budget, you create an ad or a series of ads. These are text ads of three short lines. It doesn't cost any more to run many ads, so this is an excellent place to test messages and offers, using the methods discussed in chapter 15. Ads can be grouped into campaigns and turned on and off. There are too many options to cover here, but the system is very flexible. For each ad you offer a bid, the most money you will pay each time someone clicks on this ad, and thereby visits your website. Bids start as low as a nickel per click. What makes this affordable is that you pay for clicks, not views. You are not billed for the ad being shown, only when someone clicks on it. No clicks, no cost.

If your competitor bids more than you did, his ad will run higher on the page. The key is bidding enough to stay above the fold.

Attached to each ad is a string of keywords. These are the triggers that are used to associate your ad with search results. These will come to match the keywords used on your website. I find that by using Google's keyword optimization tools and testing many different ads and keyword combinations, I can develop a set of keywords that I use on both the website and in PPC advertising.

What I really like about PPC advertising is that it is as testable as direct response. All of the major players provide extensive reporting capabilities, so that you can tell who responded to each ad variation, when, and at what cost, as well as many other variables. Because you pay only for ads that elicit a response, and because

A Special Case: Google Ad Grants

There is one tremendous free advertising resource available to nonprofits, a Google Ad Grant. These grants provide credit for AdWords advertising, which is triggered by keywords that are likely search terms. (as discussed in Chapter 12, Website 101). They are described like this on Google's website: "Google Ad Grants is the nonprofit edition of AdWords, Google's online advertising tool. Google Ad Grants empowers nonprofit organizations, through $10,000 per month in in-kind AdWords™ advertising, to promote their missions and initiatives on Google search result pages." Get more info here: www.google.com/grants/. Then go get your grant.

the reporting systems provide so much useful information, testing PPC ads are extremely effective. A a bonus, seeing which ads evoked the best response provides feedback to your entire organization, because it tells you what people were looking for when they found you. That is valuable information.

A few other ways to get into search engine results

The discussion above is about getting your name on the first page of a general search. And, really, that's the very best place to be. But search engines are many-splendored beasts, and offer many other opportunities for you to get your name and your message in front of people.

I frequently use search engines to find out what people look like, to get directions and see a neighborhood, to find merchants and services, and to get the news. Many of your constituents do too. Each of those specialized searches offer you another opportunity to get your message out.

I don't want to take too much space here to talk about secondary SEM opportunities, because I think their appropriateness to your message will be obvious. Here are a few additional paths to search engine pages:

- **Blogs & Social Sites:** Comments from or about you on these sites are often indexed.

- **Business description map placements:** Many engines will put a description of your business on a map.

- **News:** Press releases are almost always indexed when submitted through press wire services.

- **Pictures:** The pictures on your site can be indexed, as can photo sharing sites.

- **Product catalogs:** Many search engine companies also provide shopping information, including catalogs.

- **Secondary engines:** Many professional organizations and common interest groups run specialized search engines. As a bonus, these are often free.

- **Video and Podcasts:** Video and podcasts on your site or on a site like YouTube or Vimeo can be indexed.

When your site is SEO'ed and SEM'ed, and you have people visiting it in droves, a new challenge demands your attention. The next chapter talks about *stickiness,* the art and science of getting visitors to stay a while at your site.

14

Stickiness: Your Website Needs It

How to get people to stay for a while when they visit your website

Let's assume that you have optimized your website so all the search engines find it, and you've started a pay-per-click ad campaign to help bring more visitors to your site. Now, the question is, how do we direct people to what they are looking for, and what we think they will find useful. We are asking for more of our visitor's time, and getting people to give up that most precious commodity is not easy. In the web-management business, the trait of people staying awhile is called "stickiness." Your website needs to be sticky.

Analytics and Log files: the marketer's friend

Almost all web hosting services provide detailed logs of events related to your website. Google Analytics also provides much of this information. Log files tell you how many visitors have come to your site, which pages they have looked at, what browser they used, and much more. Data may be organized by time, requestor, directory, file type, or any number of other parameters. Some of these data are more important than others. Here is a list of items, along with brief descriptions, that you may find in your web server log:

- Browser used: Did your visitor use Internet Explorer, Safari, Mozilla, Chrome, or some other browser?

- Entry page: The page in your website that your visitor saw first.

- Exit Page: The page from which the visitor left your site.

- Failures: The files that were requested that could not be served. (These are called "404" errors.)

- File requests: This is a list of each file served to visitors. This is a key item – showing you exactly what people are looking at when they visit your site.

- Click path: The pages visited while on site, one after the other, from the entry page to the exit page.

- File type: A listing of files types and the number of times they were served. Types include: .html (web pages), .gif, .png and .jpg (images), .cgi (forms), .pdf (Acrobat), .mov (QuickTime movie), and many other types, depending on how your site is built.

- Hit count: The raw number of files served over some period of time.

- Referrers list: The previous site your visitor viewed.

- Source IP: The IP address of the visitor's computer. Often this is incomplete, to preserve your visitors' privacy.

- Time on site: How long the visitor stayed on your site.

- Visitor count: Also called unique viewers, this is the number of individuals who visit your site. This number will be lower than hit count, because a visitor may look at several pages, and visit more than once.

The most important of these statistics, in my opinion, are file requests, visitor count, entry and exit pages, click path, and referrer. Analysis of these data can tell you what the typical visit to your site looks like – which pages are looked at, what files are downloaded, and how long the visit lasted. These stats make it possible to tell if the things you think are important are those that your visitors look at. These stats can also tell you if a press release increased visits to your site, and by how much. These are the minimal, bottom line numbers you need to determine if your website, and particular sections and pages in it, are doing the job you expect. The other data in your web logs gives your further insight, and can be very useful as you analyze your website performance over time.

Why sticky and how sticky

Analysis of your web logs tells you how sticky your site is – that is, how long visitors stay and how many pages they look at. That obviously raises the next question: How do we make our site stickier?

I believe that there are just two keys to website stickiness: **good content** and **good navigation.**

Good content is pretty obvious. Interesting articles, enticing headlines, offers of contests or games, intriguing possibilities – these are the types of content that make people want to read more. If your website bores you, it will bore others. Make it interesting, and be sure that it is relevant and unique.

A good technique to keep your website interesting is to have frequently changing content, especially on the home page. This can be as simple as a slide show, perhaps pictures of volunteers on a project, or your staff at work. Also good is an up-to-date list of news items, a calendar of events, and ad-like sections that promote your programs. What you use will depend on your organization, but changing content encourages people to check your site frequently and increases the chance that they will find something interesting and stay awhile.

Another good way to keep people on your site is to include user involvement techniques. There is a lot of hot air being blown about on this, but essentially it means that there are interactive features that encourage visitor participation. Such features include:

- **Blogs:** A blog is simply an area where people can freely discuss whatever is on their minds. I strongly recommend that this be moderated to avoid libel, profanity, and spam. I strongly DO NOT recommend censorship of any comments simply because you disagree with them, or they conflict with what your organization thinks about an item. Free speech keeps blogs going, and people will quickly stop bothering to comment if you censor their remarks. Possibly worse – they may make a big deal of your redaction, and spread nasty remarks and rumors elsewhere on the web.

- **Video uploads and sharing:** This is a simple feature that encourages your visitors to get heavily involved in your organization. Again, be sure to look at uploaded content before it goes live to avoid embarrassment.

- **Podcasts:** these are audio files that are easy to download for offline listening on an iPod or similar device. The same rules apply – be careful about what you allow to go live, but encourage free commentary.

- **Photo sharing:** This can be a great way to have people document your event, and otherwise share good times.

Also important is good website design. Good design is another important stickiness factor. Try to look unique without being strange or off-putting. I always recommend getting a good designer and paying what that costs. A good design lasts a long time and can really help your site stand out.

I'm not going to talk much about design because it is so subjective. What I love, you may hate. A good designer will work with you, understand your audience and communications needs, and help you build a look that fits into your branding, positioning, and messaging. Those are all important parts of your System Marketing efforts.

Web designers know the ins and outs of making things look good on computer screens, which is a somewhat different science than print design. Here are a few key design factors to keep in mind:

- Make sure that your most important information is "above the fold" – showing on-screen as soon as the page loads and requiring no scrolling to be seen.

- Use a different font for headlines and text and make them big enough to read easily.

- Keep your site design narrow enough to fit on a standard screen and moderate resolution. Not everyone is using the hottest new screens, so design for the lowest common denominator. Better yet, ask your designer for a responsive design, which is one that changes aspect ratio depending on the screen it's viewed on.

- And finally, be sure to test your design on Macs, PCs and phones, and in Internet Explorer, Safari, Mozilla, Chrome, and Opera – the most used browsers.

Good navigation enables your visitor to find and go to the information she is looking for as easily as possible. Here again, a good web designer can make a great contribution by providing navigation that is easy to use, works well, and looks good. While there is no simple manual for good navigation, there are a few rules of thumb:

- Have at least two sets of navigation: top or side and bottom of the page.

- Build your main navigation so that visitors can see where they are going. Drop-down menus, or similar techniques, make it possible to see what each section of your website contains before going there. This makes navigation through your site much quicker and easier, and helps to keep your visitors from getting frustrated and leaving.

- Keep your site shallow and broad. If you diagram your site like an org chart, you want to see many second level (below the home page) choices, and you don't want to go beyond three or four levels deep. Keeping the site shallow means it takes fewer clicks to get to information, and that makes for a more satisfying experience for the visitor.

- Have a feedback mechanism that shows when a button is pushed. You can change the button color, or use sound, for example.

- Make your navigation big enough for boomers to read.

- Have a search box. Often your visitors will not know exactly where to find what they want. A good search function helps them get what they're looking for with minimal effort.

- Have an easy to find site map and be sure your site map is detailed enough to be truly useful. I think site maps should completely cover at least the top two levels of your site. The search box (that you have on every page, right?) will help people find items that are deeper than that.

Once your site has good content and good navigation, and you have optimized it for search engines, its stickiness should increase. The longer each visitor stays, the more opportunity you have to tell your story, and solicit donations. So go to it. Get sticky!

15

Testing, Testing, 1,2,3

The importance of testing your ideas and delivery, and how to do it.

How do you know what's working best in your marketing and communications? You test, test, test.

MarCom testing is the research that makes MarCom a science. You can test message, demographic selections, imagery, different media, and other options. You do this testing by setting up small, controlled experiments, and evaluating the results.

You can test almost every part of your marketing. Where to place your print advertising can be tested by running the same ad in several publications. The content of the ad can be tested by running different versions, with different response tracking, in the same publication. Website ideas can be tested by alternating web pages to see which one works better. New product ideas can be tested with focus groups. Pricing can be tested by varying prices to see if one elicits more sales. Almost any marketing idea can, and should be tested.

Direct response is one of the easiest media to test, so let's use that as an example. Direct response marketing means that you send an offer directly to your prospect, and attempt to get a response. That response could be a purchase, signing up for a newsletter, a donation, or buying tickets to an event. Direct response can be sent by email, postal mail, even a tweet.

Let me give you an example of a simple test of a direct response campaign. Keep in mind that real life testing can be much more complex than this, evaluating each part of a campaign to optimize your results. For important campaigns, I test the list, the message, the presentation, what is in the envelope, pricing, incentives, and even the color of the envelope.

In our example, we are testing the quality of our mailing list, delivery methods, and the impact of our message. The same ideas and techniques can be applied to every aspect of your effort.

Let's assume that you are tasked with raising money for a children's vaccination campaign in Tracy, California. You need to test your mailing list and your message.

Let's assume that you have available three lists of about 6,000 people each. List A is high-value donors to health campaigns in the Bay Area. List B is parents of kids in school in Tracy. List C is doctors in the Tracy area. Each list has both postal and email addresses.

We take the three lists and do what's called a random Nth name selection (choosing every 3rd, 7th, 11th, etc. name) to cut each into four groups with approximately the same number of names in it. This gives us 12 lists of 1,500 records each. Each record is coded so we know which name came from each list. (I'm assuming there are no duplicates.) We call these lists A1, A2, A3, A4, B1, B2, B3, B4, and C1, C2, C3, C4.

Now we create two message/image combinations. For example, one mailer has a picture of a sick child and the headline: "Don't let this happen to the kids in your neighborhood." Number two shows a group of mixed race children playing together. Its headline reads, "Illness doesn't recognize income, race, or gender." We create a printed and email version of each. We set up a website with a landing page for each test group.

The test runs like this. We take lists A1, B1, and C1 and email message one. To lists A2, B2, and C2, we postal mail message one. Lists A3, B3, C3 get message two in email, and the last group gets message two as postal mail. This chart illustrates the setup:

List	Message	Delivery
A1	1	Email
A2	1	Postal
A3	2	Email
A4	2	Postal
B1	1	Email
B2	1	Postal
B3	2	Email
B4	2	Postal
C1	1	Email
C2	1	Postal
C3	2	Email
C4	2	Postal

What we have done is send one of four possible message/media combinations to statistically identical groups, called cohorts. The return mailer for the postal efforts are each coded so that we know which list that person's name was on, which mailing they got, and how they got it.

We expect email response to be faster, so we send the postal mail a week before the email goes out. Now we wait. As the results start coming in, coded so that we know from which cohort and which message/media combination it came, we count. And we look for the combinations that performed best, both in terms of response and amount of donation. We wait a predetermined time, typically 2-6 weeks from the first response. And then we tabulate our results.

What we're looking for is this:

- When did the response come in? Response rates typically follow a bell curve, so this will tell us when to expect the bulk of the responses for the full effort.

- How many responded to each test variant? This tells us which combination of message, list and delivery style worked best. On a recent annual appeal, I was surprised to find that 70% of the response came from postal mailing. The previous year, response from email was much stronger.

- Who responded to each test? This will show us if people in different demographic groups or geographic locations responded differently. to different messages or delivery styles.

- What was the value of the responses from each group? Were email donations larger, or did postal mail deliver the goods? Specifically if you are soliciting donations, or selling something, this will tell you which variant provided the best ROI.

- Anything else in those numbers? Looking closely at your results may yield more information. If you tested two web pages, did one perform better? Did more women than men respond? Did particular zip codes exceed expectations? Did people seem confused or respond in unexpected ways? There's gold in them there numbers. Mine it.

When a testing is done this way, it shows you which lists perform better, which message is more persuasive, to whom you are appealing, if a particular message was more effective in postal mail or by email, and other results that you can tease out of the statistics.

Don't consider any result a failure. Testing is designed to show you what doesn't work, as well as what does. If a test fails, you've saved a lot of money and have new ideas to work with. Often, first results are ambiguous, prompting another test, or a remix of the components of the appeal.

At the end of your testing, you should have a pretty good idea of how to best communicate with your donors. Then you do your big mailing and bank your success.

16

The Best Exercise is Walking

How getting up and getting out can really boost your MarCom efforts

One of the least expensive and most effective ways of communicating about your organization is as old as campfires in the hills.

Think about how you learn about new restaurants to try, new movies to see, new bands to hear, new networks to check out. In most cases, even in our hyper-connected age, word of mouth is still the most trusted communication, especially for recommendations. Sure, we all use Yelp and TripAdvisor, but don't you usually ask your friends, too?

Getting up from your chair and getting out of the office to talk with people is one of the most cost-effective marketing arrows in your quiver.

There are a million opportunities to get out and tell people about your organization's great work. Most are free to very inexpensive. A few require larger investments, and as with any other MarCom purchase, you will evaluate their potential ROI.

Recently, as an Executive Director, I had my assistant call all of the local Rotary, Lions, and Elks clubs, as well as Chambers of Commerce, offering my services as a presenter at their frequent luncheons. Our goal was one presentation a month, and after a few weeks she had easily lined up several months worth of invitations. Not only did these talks directly bring in new business from people who had been unaware of our organization (a nonprofit social enterprise) and its great work and mission, but it enabled me to make a few long-term connections that proved to be beneficial. The cost of this? A few hours of my assistant's time and a few hours of my time. And generally speaking, I got a free lunch out of the deal. It was a good ROI.

An added benefit of these lunch-time talks was the rehearsal time they afforded me. High-level marketers are frequently required to make presentations about their organization and its programs. The Rotary lunch talks got me ready to talk to our customers, funders and donors. They helped me understand what descriptions made the best impressions and how to talk about what we did. The frequent talks showed me which jokes worked and which programs created the greatest empathy. And because I generally had a slide presentation as part of my speech, the frequent repetitions helped me fine-tune it, fixing slides that didn't flow well, or that people didn't seem to understand. After you do this a couple of dozen time, your stage fright disappears, or at least becomes controllable, and your presentations will get better and better.

Finally, the questions that always came after the prepared remarks revealed how well I was communicating, which concepts were easy to grasp and which were confusing, and what parts of our program really resonated with people. All of this was incredibly useful information, and a great opportunity to hand out business cards and brochures.

Bigger audiences, bigger opportunities

Most organizations should include conferences and conventions in their marketing efforts. These are great networking opportunities, not only simply by being there, but also by giving presentations.

There are dozens of conferences every day – you could easily spend your entire career on the road attending them. But if you pick the top two to four conferences each year and attend those, you'll make dozens of new connections and spread the word about your organization while learning new tricks from your peers.

Making presentations allows you to share your learnings. Speaking at conferences usually involves one of four presentation options: Panels, Breakout sessions, Plenaries (to everyone), and Keynotes.

Panels are conversations between two or more people on a specific topic. Audiences like these because they get a multitude of opinions addressing a specific issue. Organizers like them because they enable a lot of people to talk, and usually each speaker brings colleagues and friends to the event.

Panels can be a good way to present information, but they have a few drawbacks. Unless the moderator has good control over the panel, you can get a runaway speaker situation, where one presenter monopolizes the time available. This can be especially annoying when that presenter is not very good, or boring. Another hazard of panels is poor moderation in general. The panel moderator needs to know enough about the subject to be able to ask interesting and provocative questions, and to be able to keep the panelists on topic and on time. Panels are especially good because they give you an opportunity to get feedback from the audience. The question-and-answer period after a panel presentation is usually the most useful part of the presentation, and almost always the most interesting.

If you are asked to moderate a panel, be sure you understand the topic and the presenters as well as possible. Call the panel members beforehand, preferably in a video or audio conference so that everyone can talk together and discuss the topics you want to cover, the order of the speakers, how long each of them has for an introductory speech, whether or not you want them to use slides, and how much time you have overall. Well-run panels can be really interesting for the audience members, are great way to meet other experts in your field, and can be very rewarding.

Breakout and Plenary presentations are a bigger deal than panels, and put you in the spotlight in front of the audience, all by yourself. Breakouts take place at the same time as other sessions, and typically have only a portion of the total attendance, but otherwise are very similar to plenary sessions. Plenary presentations are usually a half hour to 45 minutes long. They require a firm understanding of your topic, a tight presentation that doesn't wander or give people time to get bored, good slides, and confidence on your part. Usually you'll work with the conference organizers to determine what the topic should be, what style of presentation they prefer, when you're going to give the presentation, and what audiovisual or other amenities will be available. This is a tremendous one-to-many communications opportunity, and a chance to share important stories about your organization's efforts, methods, and impacts.

Keynotes are often among the most highly-anticipated presentations at a conference. This gives you a huge messaging opportunity. Keynote speakers often are featured in the program and receive more attention. As with any important presentation, you want to be sure to talk to the organizers of the conference beforehand to understand their expectations, how long you have, how the stage will be set up, who you're following and preceding, and any other important details.

You may not have thought about it this way before, but keep in mind that providing a keynote presentation is often as much about entertainment as it is information exchange. This is especially true in the case of a lunch or dinner talk. You were asked to be there because your story is compelling and interesting, but you also are there to leave people feeling something. Craft your presentation to keep people enthralled. Tell a joke, if you're good at that. Make it personal, and keep it real. That opens people to hear your important message.

Before you do any presentation at a conference, or even a luncheon, be sure to rehearse it. I find it really helpful to talk to myself, rehearsing the presentation while looking at the slides, getting a sense of timing and flow. Flow is very important —your presentation has to move along as if it were a conversation. The best presentations sound like someone talking directly to you, not like someone reading a book. It takes time and practice to get relaxed enough to give a talk like that in front of an audience, and it's only possible when you know your material well.

Knowing your material does not mean reciting exactly what your slides say. People can read. Instead, use your slides to illustrate your talk. For example, a talk I used to do describing ReliaTech, a computer repair, refurbishing, and recycling nonprofit, started

What do these fellows have to do with computers? That's the question I opened some talks with.

with a full-screen, sepia-toned picture of a group of 49ers lounging by a gold mine. I would say, "While these fellows would never have imagined a personal computer, they would certainly recognize where the raw materials that make it come from." This usually got a chuckle and made people wonder how I was going to complete that connection. There were no words on that slide.

After you've talked through your presentation a few times, looking at your slides and checking how well the flow and timing works, ask a few friends to be guinea pigs and critique your presentation. I always do this before an important talk and find it to be incredibly valuable.

You don't want your friends to be just your friends when you're asking for their critique. You want them to point out the things they don't understand, and the places where you struggle with your delivery. You need them to tell you what parts of your talk are interesting, and what aren't. You need them to be brutally honest with you. This isn't the time for people to be patting you on the back, and telling you how good you are. (But you are, you're really good!)

One last thing. Don't make your presentations into commercials. Talking in a way that sounds overtly like a sales pitch is going to alienate your audience. Your presentation needs to tell the stories that help people understand your topic. It can be all about your organization and the great programs it provides. But don't make it just a sales pitch; tone it down, keep it subtle, and make it interesting. When you get people engaged with your stories, they'll be eager to learn more, eager to help, and eager to donate.

I recently saw an online conversation that started with the question, "How do I get my development director out of the office and talking to people?" Don't let your boss ever ask you that question. Whether you're in development, MarCom, or general management, get out of your chair, meet your people and tell your story.

Below is a summary of a few of the types of places you can make presentations with a few thoughts about each type of venue.

Venue	Good for	Remember
Hallway conversation at a conference	Getting to know people Practicing your elevator pitch Getting the latest gossip Learning about things before official announcements Making friends and allies	This can be the most important time at a conference. Practice your elevator pitch before you go. Notice how people react to your elevator pitch and refine it as needed.
Talks to service clubs (Rotary, Lions, Chamber of Commerce, etc.)	Getting the word out to local people. Creating new supporters Practicing your presentation skills	Wonderful practice opportunity – get your presentation down. Great way to get info to the community. Good place to meet locals who will support your mission
Panel discussion	Opportunity to tell your story Being seen as equal to other presenters (increased status) Providing short comments on a topic Learning from fellow panelists	A way onto a conference program. Often a larger audience than a service club. Connect with other presenters. Low-risk way to get feedback and test your messaging and presentation.

Continued next page.

Venue	Good for	Remember
Plenary presentation	Providing long-form information to an interested audience Establishing authority and the importance of your topic/ organization	A bigger audience with higher expectations than at a panel presentation. Keep your talk general enough to appeal to everyone. Be sure you rehearse until it becomes effortless.
Keynote presentation	Captivating an audience with the strength of your personality and the importance of your cause Being seen as important	This is the big time, be sure you are ready Remember: a keynote talk is often as much about entertainment as information. A great way to introduce new ideas, plans, efforts. By virtue of place, your status increases.

17

Making the Most of Events

Many people think that an event is a great way to raise a lot of money fast. This isn't always true.

According to my former boss and development guru, Armando Zumaya, many events, and most first events, lose money. The cost of a good event is substantial and the immediate payback from it is not always high.

He explained that the key to a successful event is to use it both as reward and cultivation opportunities. In other words, it's a place where you reward the people who have been helping you the most. The people you reward are your donors and supporters, those who have really helped you out. Not by asking them to buy a table or to support the event, but rather by giving them a table or providing recognition from the stage. You can also use events to reward your staff. Bringing staff is a great team builder and incentive. It also helps fill seats in case your event isn't the sellout you hoped for (more on that later).

There are as many types of events as there are organizations. For the purposes of this chapter, I'm thinking about an evening dinner gala. However, I think you'll find that most of these ideas apply no matter what sort of event you are producing.

Armando explained that the highest value of your event is cultivation. Cultivation means talking to people who may give to your organization in the future, or who may increase the amount of their ongoing support. Events do this by providing an entertaining program that helps them feel good, meet other supporters, better understand the organization, and see how well run it is.

It's essential to demonstrate competence, because the impression that people get from your event is going to carry over to their feelings about the entire organization. Think about your reaction when you have a great server at a restaurant. The food tastes better. Likewise, if the service is bad it leaves you less excited about the food. The impression you leave with is dependent on the totality of your experience.

Enveloping your planning for the event itself is all the promotional and impact planning, as well as establishing measurement points for evaluating the event. Your event planning should start with concrete and measurable goals. Those goals might include

developing five new major donors, or having X number of City Council members attend. Your goals may include a monetary target, such as raising $100,000. It's important to have all the goals in mind because this will guide the event planning, and allow you to make informed decisions on the budget and on which ideas contribute to the overall impact of the event. After the event, they provide the measuring stick against which you evaluate the event's success.

Event planning as part of Systems Marketing

Let's think about how events connect to your total marketing effort. In an organization with Systems Marketing thinking, event planning would start early. A year in advance is not too soon to start thinking about a large event. Annual events are often on staff work plans as a year-round effort, because there's always some preparatory activity to do, and there's always follow-up work. A Systems Marketing organization knows that a big event is going to impact virtually everybody in the organization.

Every event should have a planning committee that is made up of people from the various departments that are affected by the event or contribute to it. These people are conduits for information from their teams to and from the event committee. Obviously the communications team has to get the word out early and often, and plan follow-up.

The event committee needs to keep in mind all aspects of the event. The planning checklist varies a lot, but will include things like securing a venue, building the guest list, catering, decorations, designing and printing the program, door prizes, promotion, program, and, if you have an auction, arranging for donations for it, as well as the many other items critical to the success of the event. That is just for the event itself. As you can see from that list, which is nowhere near complete, there's an awful lot of moving parts related to pulling off the big event. At one event I worked on, we produced a nine-minute video that took three months to produce. It's important to do your planning in advance, and understand the time and the budget.

It's also important to evaluate what you can do in-house and what you want to outsource. Catering is an obvious task that is usually best to contract out. AV production, decorating, design and printing are other aspects of events that are often handed off to contractors. Be realistic in balancing your resources – some things you can and should do in house, some things should be outsourced.

The event committee needs to work closely with your communications department to make sure that the branding of the event, including its name and logo, are appropriate both to the event and to the larger branding of the organization. It's possible to completely confuse your audience by mixing up your messages. A clear purpose and messaging are essential to garner positive attention and attendance.

Often the development team is the lead team on event planning because it's so critical to their work. As we discussed earlier, donor cultivation is a major goal of many events. This is where the development team shines. Events give the development team an opportunity to personally reach out to major donors. They also enable fund raising from corporate and foundation supporters, who will buy tables and sponsorships. It's an opportunity to raise money through raffles and auctions, and thereby a chance to reach out to in-kind donors who will provide the items that you offer. The development team will also see your event as an opportunity to invite people who haven't donated, so they can see what your organization is all about.

It's very important for the development team to be thinking about goals and accountability related to the event. If your goal is to invite 20 new potential donors, sell 12 tables, and raise $15,000, you need to write those goals down and measure the appropriate data to determine whether or not you've hit your targets. This is easy when you build in specific points to measure at the planning stage.

The event

Let's plan a hypothetical event and take a look at what it takes to make the event work well. Our hypothetical organization is *Kitty Rescue League*. Kitty Rescue League collects feral cats, neuters them, and releases them or finds them adoptive homes. The hopefully-annual Fat Cat Bash is being attempted for the first time. The goals are to bring in 20 potential new donors, raise $10,000, and recognize existing donors.

In order to raise interest and recognize major supporters, Kitty Rescue League is going to make several awards to people or organizations that have significantly helped to save kitties in the past year.

The Fat Cat Bash budget

Kitty Rescue League has a mailing list of approximately 3,500 names. They're hoping that they can get 5% of that list, or 175

About awards

Why do so many organizations give so many awards? It's not a conspiracy by the trophy industry. Awards are a great way to gain positive attention, recognize your donors and others in the community, and give your organization a topic for a good press release. Awards bring in the recipients and their friends and families. They increase interest, and rightfully bestow recognition on those who work hard for your cause.

Awards don't have to be extravagant to be appreciated. A nice trophy, an engraved clock, or some similar memento says thank you over and over. No one gets all the attention they need or deserve; your organization can make its donors feel great by recognizing them at an annual event, where the community can hear about their good deeds and express its appreciation.

people, to come to their bash. So now the planning team needs to create a budget that shows how to pay for the cost of the event and show a profit.

Kitty Rescue League's budget for the Fat Cat Bash looks like this:

As you can see, even if Kitty Rescue League meets their attendance goals, they miss their revenue target. That means that the

EXPENSES		INCOME	
Space Rental	$1,500	Tickets, 175 at $75	$13,125
Catering, 200	5,000	Sponsorships	20,000
Audio/visual	1,500	Program ads	1,000
Printed programs		Total	$34,125
& favors	875		
Program	15,000		
Marketing	5,000	**NET**	$3,250
Decorations	1,000		
Total	$29,875		

planners need to decide if they want to proceed with a smaller return.

Looking at this budget, the event committee has several options. They can change their goals, they can reduce the cost of the event, or they can figure out a way to bring in more revenue.

Key to making this evaluation is determining the higher priority: long-term or immediate revenue. If cultivation (long-term revenue) is more important, it may make sense to run the event expecting a low return, or even to take a loss, in order to have the opportunity to meet and interact with the people that they need to talk with. If revenue is a prime goal then it is important to look at both sides of the budget to see where costs can be reduced or income grown. For example, the $15,000 cost for the program includes creating a video presentation of the award winners. Perhaps money could be saved by instead doing a montage of still pictures which would require no original taping. Or maybe a video production company can be found that would donate part or all of the cost of production. Other expenses should be looked at too, but it's always best to start with your biggest expense, because that's where you're most likely to find some fat to trim.

On the income side of the table, there aren't very many options. Calculating the increase in donations resulting from the dinner will help, but is a very unreliable figure. Kitty Rescue League can charge more for tickets, but that may make it more difficult to get people there. Additional sponsorships may be possible and it may also be possible to raise the cost of advertising in the program to raise more money there. Maybe adding a raffle or auction would increase revenue, but with additional costs that have to be figured in. Perhaps bigger actually works better than smaller. Because your expenses do not go up directly with the number of attendees, it may make sense to increase seats to 200 or 300. However the challenge then becomes getting those additional people to the event, which typically would require increased marketing and communication costs, and often more staff time.

That brings up the importance of filling seats. Nothing is worse than a partially empty banquet hall. It is far better to oversell a small event, and bring in extra tables, then to undersell the room. You may have the same number of people there, but the packed room looks infinitely better. This where your staff can help out. A good rule of thumb, if your staff is large enough, is to have one staff person at each table. Board members also can help with this usually pleasant assignment. They can answer questions about your organization and help make your guests feel welcome. But staff and board members and their (adult) families can also help fill seats to ensure that the room is filled to capacity. It is a nice reward to invite your staff, and they will help your event succeed simply by being there.

The Program

What is going to happen at the Fat Cat Bash? You don't want people to simply come in, eat and leave. So a program is in order.

First, don't overdo the program. 30-45 minutes is usually enough. If you run late, people become impatient. If you are boring, it's even worse.

The program needs to be both entertaining and interesting. Again, an award ceremony, if it is appropriately brief, is a great way to create excitement and enthusiasm. A door prize drawing does the same. Perhaps Kitty Rescue League has connections to a musical act, or a staff member who is a good magician. Adding entertainment to the bill can be very enjoyable. But again, be sure the entertainers, unless they're cute children, are professional enough to entertain, and not embarrass.

A keynote speaker is often considered de rigueur at nonprofit event. This can be good or bad. Some very impressive and effective people are not good presenters. Some speakers enjoy their own voices so much you almost have to drag them off the stage. Either of these situations can really bring down the mood and wreck your schedule.

If you want to have a keynote speaker, find someone who knows your organization and can say nice things about it. Have someone see them present before you book them to ensure that they will provide a good presentation. If at all possible, get someone with name recognition, a person who will help you sell tickets.

Finally, don't forget the ask. No one is going to be offended by having your Executive Director or Development Director make a brief pitch. People are there because they care. So Kitty Rescue League will tell them about the tremendous impact they've had over the past year, some of the challenges facing the organization, and how X more dollars will make a huge difference in the coming year. For added impact, place a donation envelope under each plate.

After the event

After the event, there are two important tasks – follow-up and evaluation.

Follow-up means that your event and development teams get on the phone and call people to thank them for attending. Nothing cements a relationship like a personal touch. There are entire books on cultivating donors, but suffice it to say that you need many touches with each donor, and your post-event phone call is an important one. That is when you can ask for support, get feedback on the event, and stay in touch with the people who keep you going. I can't overemphasize the importance of this step in funder cultivation.

Thank your in-kind and other donors who helped you stage your event. Again, your personal attention is worth a lot, don't be stingy with it.

I recommend that you follow up your event with a press release that describes how well the Bash went, how much money was raised, what dignitaries attended, whatever else is important, and announces the date of next year's event.

Finally, a few days after the event (when people have had a chance to catch up on their sleep) get the event team together for a post mortem. What went well? What would you do differently? What was awful? Be honest and fair. Evaluate the work plan, the promotional efforts, and your vendors. Take notes and refer to them before your next event. Only through an honest appraisal will you be able to improve on your event.

This chapter addressed planning for a dinner event, but planning for any other type of event is not dissimilar. Obviously, a 5K run has different details, but the process is similar.

Events can be a lot of fun, good money-raising opportunities, and ways to acknowledge the people that help you carry out your mission. But they are complex and important, so do the work up front, and then enjoy your event. As my old boss always said, "Have fun kids!"

18

Writing the Press Release that People Read

In my many years as a journalist and editor, half the press releases I've ever received were tossed away after I read the first sentence. Half of those left were deep-sixed when I finished the first paragraph. Half of the rest were filed. Will your press release land in the recycling bin or on the front page?

Thanks to social media, press release are less important these days, but for really important announcement, you should send them to your media list.

The secrets of writing good press releases are not dissimilar to those of any good writing. You have to be relevant. You have to catch the reader's attention. You have to spell well and write coherent sentences. Most of all, you have to write about something interesting.

Determining what is interesting is where many people seem to have problems. I've seen hundreds of press releases touting the latest upgrade to an obscure piece of software, or the recent promotion of someone I have never heard of, working for a company of equal obscurity. What these releases have in common is their lack of a hook – the bit of information that catches my eye, and makes me want to know more.

What they also have in common is a lack of understanding of the recipient. Your organization's hiring of a new development director will not interest a vast audience, but it will interest other nonprofit leaders, foundation program managers, and large donors. So the key is to put the information in front of them – the people who care about your news.

Another all too common foible of PR writing is the overuse of jargon. I have gotten dozens of releases that start out like this: "XYZ Corporation Announces New Breakthrough in FPGA Speed – Attains 128MIPS with new AGX-SSP1405." This is typically followed by a series of acronyms and abbreviations, interspersed with words that look vaguely like English. Even in a highly technical marketplace (where I have spent a lot of time), this sort of language is a turn-off and is certain to accomplish little other than filling recycling bins. Nonprofits can be equally incomprehensible. My advice is to keep your language intelligent and simple. Imagine that you are explaining the topic to your father. Making it easy to understand will not insult the cognoscenti, but will give you a chance to influence the people who are not experts in your field.

Writing a good news release, like any other writing task, is a combination of inspiration and skill. These points will help you understand the skills you need. If you keep these seven items in mind, your press releases will work hard for you.

1: **Know your audience.** How often do you think the editor of a computer graphics technical magazine will print articles on new women's clothing? Having held that position, I can assure you that the answer is "never." However, I frequently got press releases on clothing and fashion, new music players, new food products, great real estate opportunities, and incoming executives in the banking industry. My total interest in those releases was equal to the likelihood of my publishing them – zero. More importantly, the communications people and PR agencies that sent them got demerits for wasting my time. If you want to keep on the good side of journalists and editors (trust me, you do.) do your homework and build of list of media contacts who are interested in your story and clients. Otherwise, you're wasting your time and theirs.

2: **Sell the story.** Journalists have a job to do, which is meeting their readers' needs for information. To do that, they have to sell story ideas to their editors. You have to sell your story to the reporter or editor to whom you send it. This person is a gatekeeper – and their work is easier if they keep the gate shut and just say no. But they need material and they need to address the interests of their readers. So, know the journalists, know the readers, and be prepared to pitch the story on their terms – make it easy for the gatekeeper to say yes. You do that by having clear objectives. When you know the answers to those questions, you are ready to write a good release:

- What do we want them to know about us?

- How do we want them to feel about us?

- How do we want to be perceived by them?

3: **Remember the five W's.** Do you remember the five W's? As a reminder, they are:

- Who

- What

- When

- Where

- Why

Every story needs to include this information. A strong

lead paragraph (more on this below) will include the 5 W's right at the top. Be sure that you include these items so your readers will get what they need quickly.

4: **Make the headline catchy.** I think a creative headline can help the weakest story. And it won't hurt a strong release to have an eye-catching headline. If we think about our example of an organization that helps Central American farmers, imagine that they issue a press release talking about the impact their program has had in El Salvador. The release is written, but a discussion arises about the headline. Headline one is, "Aid and education help farmers increase yields in El Salvador." Headline two says, "El Salvador child deaths plummet thanks to better nutrition." Which story would you read first?

5: **Write a strong lead.** The lead is the first sentence or two of an article. A strong lead pulls the reader in and makes that reader want to know more. A good headline catches the reader's (and editor's) eye; a strong lead invites them to finish the story. To follow the headline we discussed above, we might write a lead like this: "In 1999, 40% of El Salvador's poor children died from nutritionally-linked diseases or starvation. Last year, after [our group] taught El Salvador's farmers better methods, child deaths from nutritional problems are down more than 78%." Don't you want to know more about that now?

6: **Write a story, not an ad.** A PR is not advertising, and that needs to be clear in your planning and writing. A big difference is intent – a news release is intended to form the basis of a story. Ad copy is intended to sell something. A PR is informative, an ad is persuasive. Good editors do not print ad copy presented as a story. Your release needs to contain information. It needs to inform and interest the reader. It needs to create an emotional response. Save your hard-sell pitch for your ads. Tell a story in your news release.

7: **Skip the CEO's quote.** Among journalists, quotes from the CEO are some of the biggest jokes going. Editors know the CEO is proud of this accomplishment and hopes to continue this positive trend. We know she is thrilled to death to be teaming up with JKL Company and that this will probably be the most important product release since the serpent's apple in Eden. So don't waste your paper and the reporter's time with this drivel if at all possible. If your CEO really has something interesting or important to say, that's great. If your product just killed 100 customers, the CEO had better make a statement. If the CEO is the subject of the story – for example, she just won a big prize – then let's hear her comments. Otherwise, let the CEO relax at a board retreat, and give the public some real information instead.

Finally you need to pitch your release. That means that you write a strong but brief cover letter that explains why your story is important, who will want to read it, and why a particular media outlet is the right place for the story. If this is a really important story, you may want to offer an exclusive to a few reporters. If you do so, do it sequentially, to one at a time. And be careful to live up to your promise. Remember, only one reporter gets an exclusive.

After you send your letters and releases, wait a few days and then call the people you sent them to. Talk to the reporters about your organization, your story, and their readers. This is when you are selling your story – and good reporters will appreciate hearing about good stories. They may ask for more information, photos, or an interview. Be ready to provide what they need quickly. Ask them what their deadline is, and respect it. Deadlines do not get stretched in the media business, so if you help reporters meet their deadlines you will get far better coverage.

19

About Advertising

Advertising. We are all surrounded by it, inundated by aural and visual noise that pollutes our environment and covers every surface around us. In the United States, an urban dweller can easily be subjected to 5,000 advertising messages every day. But advertising serves a purpose and the best advertising sticks in our minds for years. Good advertising reaches the right audience with the right story at the right time. Good advertising creates good impressions and memories. There's no reason that you shouldn't use advertising to help get your message out. The only question is how to advertise so that your advertising meets the two primary measures of effectiveness:

1: Reaching the right people with the right message, and

2: Doing that while spending as little money as possible.

As with any other marketing, you first have to understand your audience. You should already know your audience fairly well. You should have lots of information on your donors, as well as people who have expressed an interest. You should also have good records for your clients, who often can become donors and supporters as their situations change. You have a clear mission and vision, and a well-crafted message.

As in any other marketing effort, you first want to define your goals. What are you trying to accomplish with this advertising? Who do you need to reach? What do you want them to do? How much money do you have to spend? How long do you have to accomplish your goals?

As part of your System Marketing plan, advertising needs to fit in with all the other marketing that you're doing. Everything needs to form a coherent whole. Your staff needs to be ready to handle inquiries and be prepared to respond quickly to people who are interested in your product. Depending on the product you're promoting — whether it be your big annual benefit, a donor outreach effort, a new program, a new service or product from your social enterprise — the entire advertising campaign, including preparation for response, needs to be thought out in advance, with data collection and measuring points built-in.

One of things to remember about advertising is that one ad rarely is as effective as you hope it will be. People respond to repetition. They need to see your ad over and over again. Big advertisers are aware of this. Think about how often you've seen the GEICO gecko. So before your event you should run the same ad, or very similar ads, in as many places, as many times as you can afford. Newspapers and online outlets provide regular updates which enable you to have many impressions in the window of time available. More impressions are good. Just be sure you're reaching the people you need to get your message.

Let's consider a hypothetical case, an advertising campaign to support Kitty Rescue League's Fat Cat Bash. The goal of this at this event is to bring a hundred seventy-five donors to a fancy dinner. The advertising budget is $2,000. That might not seem like a lot of money but we will see how to spend it to get the most effective return.

Identifying our target demographic is fairly easy. We know we want to reach cat lovers in our local area. We know that older cat lovers have greater disposable income, and possibly more free evenings. However, we don't want to ignore the significant millennium generation; a lot of them like cats too.

We start by surveying local media: radio, TV, newspapers, and magazines. For each of these we want to ask publishers to provide demographic as well as distribution information. For example, where I live, the San Francisco Chronicle is the largest newspaper, reaching close to half a million people every day. Its distribution range is roughly a 200 mile diameter from its publishing base in San Francisco. If I needed to reach a lot of people who didn't need to be in any particular nearby area, the Chronicle is a great way to do it. However the Kitty Rescue League is in a small suburb of San Francisco. Ninety percent of their donors live within twenty-five miles of the office. So buying advertising in the Chronicle would not be cost-effective, because much of the advertising would be wasted on people who live too far away. Looking further, the marketing intern at Kitty Rescue League discovers that a local weekly newspaper covers the target geographic area well and has a broad demographic appeal. This newspaper fits the requirements very well and happily, it costs far less than the Chronicle.

Other local advertising opportunities might include church newsletters, local animal shelters' newsletters, and newsletters at nearby senior centers. All of these are relatively inexpensive. Because this is a one-time event your campaign will only stretch over a month or two, which also reduces cost. What is important is reaching the target demographic, and reaching a lot of people a number of times, while staying within your budget.

For radio and TV, be sure to consider public service announcements (PSA's). They can be provided by email, or, if you have the ability to produce it, a complete video announcement. Be sure to contact the stations directly to learn how they handle PSA's. PSA's are free, but you have no control over when, or even if, they are broadcast. If you do create a video, be sure you also post it on social media sites.

However, print and TV are far from your only advertising options. Social media is an essential part of your advertising mix, especially for fast-breaking information. Social media is also very inexpensive – essentially free – so you can use it a lot with minimal impact on your budget. Remember though, that the criteria for social media must be evaluated in the same way as those for print: reach and audience are key items to look at. Social media can cast a broad net, or can be tightly targed by a variety of demographic options. If it's free it doesn't matter that much of the reach is wasted. But when you pay for social media, such as Facebook ads, be certain you reaching the right people, in the right places. Remember too, that social media is ephemeral and dynamic, so you must update it frequently, and you must keep your updates interesting or you risk losing your audience.

Online advertising is another important option to consider. Online ads can appear as banners or blocks on websites, in emails and on social media sites. Search engine advertising (discussed in Chapter 21) can provide visibility in the right places. Like any other advertising, online ads need to be an intentional part of the marketing mix, carefully planned to augment your other marketing efforts and carefully tracked and evaluated.

Here's a checklist of things to think about as you plan your advertising:

- The demographics of your target audience, including gender, age, income, physical location, previous giving history, and other pertinent information.

- Specific program interests, which means that certain donors prefer to engage with certain programs.

- Media preferences. For example if most of your

donors are under 30, mobile media might be the way to reach them best. However if your donors are older and perhaps not as computer literate, you may reach them best on traditional media; television, radio, newspapers, and magazines.

- Budget. You don't want to spend more than you can afford.

- An offer. What's your call to action? You need to get people to do something; for example, buy tickets for the Fat Cat Bash.

- Set goals. What do you want your ads to achieve? What will you measure to gauge response?

Measuring response in advertising is pretty simple. You can create a webpage with no menu links and direct people to it. (This is called a "landing page.") You can have a sign-up form on your website dedicated to collecting responses to your ads. You can establish a special email address. Other options are coupons – people like discounts, offer codes, and the very simple phrase, "mention this ad for…" Coach the people who answer your phones to ask, "How did you hear about us/this event/this program?" and record the answers you get. Below is source tracking worksheet I developed for a retail social enterprise.

Finally, be sure your budget includes a good graphic designer for your print and online efforts. Your audience is sophisticated and will ignore or deride bad design. The money you spend for good design will help your organization look professional and help your advertising cut through the noise. Ultimately, that's your bottom line.

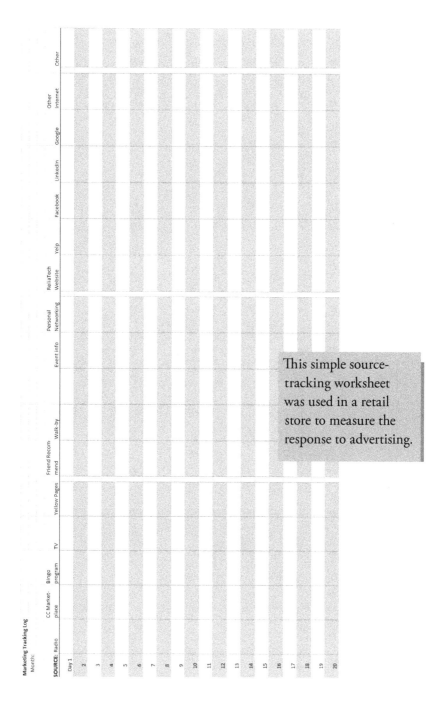

Marketing Tracking Log
Month:

SOURCE:	Radio	CC Market-place	Bingo program	TV	Yellow Pages	Friend Recommend	Walk-by	Event info	Personal Networking	ReliaTech Website	Yelp	Facebook	LinkedIn	Google	Other Internet	Other
Day 1																
2																
3																
4																
5																
6																
7																
8																
9																
10																
11																
12																
13																
14																
15																
16																
17																
18																
19																
20																

This simple source-tracking worksheet was used in a retail store to measure the response to advertising.

20

What to Measure, Why and When

Research, Assessment, and Evaluation

How many meetings have you attended in which the term "data-driven" was tossed about, its utter essentiality stressed?

And how many times did you have the feeling that no one in the room had a clue what "data-driven" really means?

As one who has made a living doing market research, I learned to like data. Now, I just love data. One of my greatest thrills at work in a social enterprise was finally discovering a seasonal cycle in the sales at our store. This information helped us plan a sale at the right time that doubled the store receipts that month. That's an example of data-driven decision making.

I can't provide you with a course on statistics. Even if I were qualified to do so, we don't have the space for that level of detail. What I do hope to provide is a framework for thinking about data and evaluation that will make your work a bit easier.

Data doesn't just measure results

I think it is very important to use data to shape programs, both in initial planning and through a reiterative, ongoing analysis. Changes are driven by the findings, and often answering one question raises other questions.

Data-driven programs work this way:

- Program planning is based on research, with measurement points built in, plus

- Ongoing, reiterative analysis of the collected data is used to refine the program and deepen understanding, then

- Programs are changed as new knowledge emerges from the data.

That is what a true data-driven organization does.

It takes rigor and discipline to work this way, but the resulting improvements in programs designed like this are worth the effort. That's why all major retailers use a similar model, as pioneered by Wal-Mart.

Using Data

Include milestones and measurement points in your plan.

Carefully evaluate the results against your expectations.

Revise your plan based on the data you collect.

Planning for data

The very first thing to consider when planning for assessment is what you need to know, and why. Having a clear picture of how the information you collect will positively impact your organization makes the process easier and enables good decisions as you design your research and evaluation protocol.

Key in determining what you want to know is evaluating your questions in regard to their impact on your program and the ability to collect meaningful data.

For example, a hypothetical child nutrition advocacy organization, which we'll call Kids.org, is planning a new child nutrition program. Their questions include: What is the dietary value of the average child's meals? Does smoking in the home affect a child's appetite? What foods are both nutritious and appealing to kids? If these are significant issues, what Kids.org programs will impact them positively?

There are five concerns that must be addressed when creating the Kids.org assessment plan. Let's address each of the five key aspects of their, or your, assessment plan.

1: What do we need to know, and why?

Assuming that good nutrition promotes good health and better learning, Kids.org wants to know the following about the kids it serves:

- What is the dietary value of the average child's meals? Are they getting enough of what they need? Are any key nutrients missing from their diet?

- Does smoking in the home affect a child's appetite? If so, is there a correlation with illness or learning/ behavioral issues?

- What foods are nutritious, inexpensive, and appealing to kids? What can we afford to provide that the kids will like and is good for them?

2: What information will tell us what we need to know?

- What do the kids eat during some period of time.
- A census of smokers in the children's homes.
- Health and school records for the children
- A list of affordable, nutritious foods, taste tested with the kids.

3: Has anyone already answered this question?

- There may be studies available to provide dietary information that is good enough. It will be hard to have enough diaries completed to gather significant data.
- Most likely, Kids.org will have to find the smokers' houses though a questionnaire or personal contact with the parents.
- Are there existing studies on the impact of smoking in the home on children's health and behavior?
- Nutritional information for the foods Kids.org can afford is easily obtained. Taste testing can take place by evaluating orders for food, or servings eaten, and by asking questions.

4: How do we collect the data we need?

- Data may be found from online sources, including government, universities, journals, and general web searches.
- Online, written, phone, or personal surveys.
- A detailed diary may be required to track eating habits.
- Measuring and tracking food ordered over time. Frequently interacting with clients to ask what they think of the food, your organization, how you do business, and more.

5: How will we analyze the data to inform our future actions?

- Does someone on staff know enough to collect and analyze the data? Offices that use programs like SalesForce and QuickBooks can output reports into Excel for analysis. Many CRM/accounting systems offer advanced and customizable reporting to provide much of the data you need.

- A local college or business school may be able to provide interns who understand how to manipulate data to find the information you need. It's important to have these interns carefully document their methods and cross train staff to take over when the intern leaves.

- Reporting experts can be hired on contract to periodically provide the information you need from your data.

Once you have the information you sought, you can modify your programs to be even more effective. Kids.org finds that there are many reports on average child diets in various locations, including a city near them that has very similar demographics. A quick check with a few of their clients indicated that their clients were eating pretty much what that study reported. It showed that kids ate too much sugar and salt, and not enough fruits and veggies. Kids.org starts an education campaign while also finding particular foods that provide needed nutrients.

Existing research enables Kids.org to find that smoking in the house has a negative impact on kids. Kids.org starts providing information for parents to explain the importance of a smoke-free environment for their kids. They continue to measure smoking versus achievement to determine the impact of the smoke-free program, and modify it until it has the desired impact.

Kids.org also changed their food offerings and started requesting different foods from their donors. They discover that small variations in sourcing can make significant improvements in child nutrition.

Data collection and evaluation continues for the life of the program. It enables adjustments that provide continuous improvement in the program delivery, reduction of costs, and increasingly better outcomes.

Added benefits

Not only does Kids.org have a better understanding of its clients, it also has better impact data, and is able to make some changes based on what was found in the data. They collect data continuously, and evaluate it periodically to assess their work. In the future, they may find that their data includes answers to other questions that hadn't been asked at the onset of the program. Kids.org better understands how and why their programs work, providing greater insight and impact, which, by the way, will also please their funders.

All of this applies equally well to marketing. You can, and should, design all of your marketing campaigns with measuring points built in. You can count clicks, calls, and customers. With tools like Google Analytics and AdWords, Twitter hashtags, specialized landing pages and other tools, you can evaluate the success of online campaigns. Online marketing can change by the minute as new data arrive. Response to print ads, direct response, and press releases can be measured and efforts refined. Obviously, donations provide their own inherent measurement systems, but even in fund raising you can measure other variables that enable you to better craft your message and delivery to improve giving.

The bottom line is the bottom line. No matter how you measure your success, whether it is families helped, revenue from a social venture, kilowatts saved, jobs created, or new money raised, you can determine significant measuring points. By taking frequent readings, and acting on the data you collect, you can make any organization work better and have greater impact.

21

Open in case of emergency

Managing communications in a crisis

It's bound to happen. One of your major funders cuts you off. Your ED is accused of sexual harassment. The CFO makes off with your bank account. There's a fire in your office. You've been hacked and your client records are exposed. Your reputation is at stake. Your funding is at stake. Every nonprofit may have to deal with problems like these at some time. How you deal with them can make a substantial difference in the health of your organization, and indeed, whether or not your organization survives.

Dealing with situations like these is called *Crisis Management*. How you handle a crisis is vitally important. Every member of the leadership team needs to be aware and involved, and those in Marketing and Communications can be vital to a successful resolution of the situation. In this chapter I'm going to offer a few tips, some of which are based on my personal experience managing communications during crisis.

First an anecdote. At a community-based organization (CBO), a surprise inspection by the fire marshall resulted in a notice to abate (meaning that they had to correct any problems with the building or cease operations). The landlord, the Board of Directors and the staff were near panic. What was going to happen? They had 5000 square feet full of stuff, a staff of 11, and limited resources.

"Information" got out quickly and created an immediate ruckus. One long-term volunteer started telling clients that the organization would soon close. She advised the staff to start looking for new jobs. Customers and staff alike were asking how long the organization would be in business and what its fate would be.

This was a classic example of the need to manage the message. The leadership team had to respond to the people who were calling, writing, tweeting, and emailing, all with increasing concern about the fate of the organization. A local newspaper ran an article with a headline announcing that the CBO was about to be evicted. All of this happened over a couple of weeks, and created an intense sense of urgency.

While this organization did not have a written crisis management plan, crisis management had been given a lot of thought and discussion. I don't recommend being that casual, but that is, at the minimum, where to start with your own crisis management and communications planning.

The Board knew about the Order to Abate before the newspaper article appeared. Knowing that the situation sounded ominous, they went to work crafting a comprehensive, coherent and consistent message that everyone would use when talking about the situation. The Board worked on this message for several days, consulting by way of email and phone calls, until a short message that was accurate, truthful and calming was agreed upon. Immediately, the message was used in consistent response to emails and posted on social media accounts and the organization's website.

In addition, the organization added a page to their website where they posted news and allowed the community to comment and talk among themselves. A GoFundMe campaign was started in response to the many people who had asked what they could do to help.

This turned out to be a successful example of how thinking about crisis communication management before an event occurs makes it easier to respond. Because the leadership team had started working on messaging early, the communications were effective, the panic quelled, the GoFundMe page raised several thousand dollars, and time was extended for compliance with the order.

Are you ready to handle a crisis? Let me share a few tips on handling communications during a crisis.

Don't wait for an emergency.

"You have to anticipate a crisis in order to deal with it when it comes."
Daniel Kennedy, PR and MarCom authority

One of the most important aspects of dealing with a crisis is being ready for it. It is far easier to think about your emergency response in the calm before the storm.

An organizational crisis management plan should be prepared by every nonprofit. Developing this plan should be a collaborative effort involving your leadership team, the Board of Directors and other key stakeholders in your organization. The plan should include what to do in various types of emergencies, such as a fire, an earthquake, a tornado, a serious injury, a broken pipe or a heart attack, as well as unexpected media coverage or allegations about the organization, whether true or not. It should include a list of contact information for the people who may need to be reached in case of emergencies, such as the police, the fire department, your landlord, your insurance broker and others. Your plan should include managing clients at your site, evacuation procedures (and what triggers them), and other aspects of likely, and unlikely, events at your organization. Of course, you want to be certain that your overall crisis management plan recognizes the differing requirements of various situations and addresses them.

Your crisis management plan should be easily accessible and should be reviewed at least once a year to make sure that it is still up-to-date and appropriate. In the case of some types of emergencies you will want to have periodic drills to help the staff understand how to respond in various situations.

Every comprehensive crisis management plan should include a crisis communications section. It's important to coordinate with your leadership team to make sure that communications efforts align with and augment the crisis management plans that have been adopted. It's also vital that you are prepared to defend your reputation and to show that you are handling the situation well.

Let's look at what your Crisis Communications Plan should include.

Crisis Communications Plan Checklist

Start with a general plan, and then think of special situations and what they will require. Here are some of the key items to include in your crisis communications plan:

- The person, or people, who are authorized to speak publicly about an event or situation. Typically, designated members of the Board, the Executive Director, and/or a media specialist are the only people authorized to make public statements. Everyone else in the organization, including Board members and staff, should refer questions to the designated spokespeople. This is a "must do" and is critically important.

- Try to anticipate the various types of situations that may arise. For example, there may be workplace violence, or a serious injury at the work site.

There could be a fire, explosion, or leak of toxic materials. There could be a natural disaster, like a hurricane, tornado, earthquake or flood. There could be accusations of sexual or other harassment. Malfeasance on the part of your Board or staff leadership can occur, or merely be alleged. These types of situations, as well as the ones that are unique to your organization or location, should be evaluated, and appropriate responses prepared for those that are most likely.

- List the people or teams that will be gathering information and how that information will be provided to the communications team. Include people to talk with: an attorney, an insurance broker, an HR expert, or a CPA, for example. The board and staff leadership should develop an approval process, and that process should be evaluated periodically. The plan will include the approvals needed before releasing information.

- Your communication strategy should incorporate the right media for the situation: social media, your website, traditional media, external and internal communications channels. One of the biggest advantages of having a crisis communications plan is that your message placement is predetermined, enabling you to act quickly and avoid bad decisions. Even so, remember that every situation is unique, with unique communication needs. You'll often have to adjust on the fly.

- Include a list of local journalists that you want to contact. List each with the topic/beat he or she covers. Be sure you have your statement ready before you contact the press, and get it first to those who have been friendly to your organization.

- In addition, have a list of your other stakeholders that you'll want to contact in various situations, before you go public, if possible. For example, if there's a fire, you may need to contact your staff and clients right away. As you draw up this list, consider priorities: who do you contact first, second, and on down the list? If there's a political situation, you may want to contact your local representatives or department heads with whom you do business. Think about your bankers, funders, individual donors, advisory board, and anyone else who needs to hear what is happening directly from the organization. Be ready with an elevator pitch for Board and staff to use casually. Keep in mind that your loyal supporters can help spread your message – draft them as ad hoc boosters, and keep them informed of changes in the situation and the official messaging. This is a critical element in your plan for successfully handling a situation.

- You also want to think about how you're going to get information to your staff. Think about what will be necessary if they are at work, or not, and be ready to let them know what's going on, and what is expected of them. Warn them against speaking to anyone, especially the media, about what is happening. Instead, emphasize that they should refer questions to the authorized spokespersons.

What to do when they unexpected occurs

Your communications plan gives you a head start on how you will be communicating in the event of a crisis. However, it's impossible to preplan what you're going to say. These pointers will help you be prepared when you need to act quickly. But remember – the situation will change, and you need to be ready for the unexpected.

- **Get the facts. Then act thoughtfully.**
  When a crisis is upon you, you need to get in front of the story as quickly as possible, and you need to do

that in a thoughtful way. Approach your information-gathering from a journalist's point of view: Who, What, Where, When, and Why. Use those questions to guide you as you collect facts. Don't jump to conclusions. Check back with people as the situation changes. They may have new information, and you may have new questions. Be sure you understand the situation and be aware that it may change rapidly. Stories evolve and change – everyone expects that. But retractions or major corrections can hurt credibility.

- **Identify the people who are directly affected by the situation.**
  It's important to understand who the audience and stakeholders are in any given situation. Sometimes you need to collect information from them, sometimes you need to get information to them. Knowing your audience and stakeholders in any given situation is critical to effective communications. Develop lists of likely stakeholders and audiences who will have or need information in various situations.

- **Get expert help.**
  Don't rely just on yourself and your in-house team in a crisis situation. You may need to consult an attorney. You may want to talk with your insurance agent. You may have other stakeholders who can help due to specific knowledge of the situation or expertise in a specific domain.
  Be sure you talk to your experts before you craft your statement, because what they say might directly impact what you say. Remember, though it may evolve over time as the situation changes, you have only one chance to get the first message correct, and to get in front of the situation.
  Develop a list of advisors who you will contact in various situations.

- **Work with your board and the other people directly involved to arrive at a consensus on messaging. Then, craft a statement that you will use consistently to explain the situation.**
  Once you are confident that the situation is understood, and stakeholders identified, work together to determine how you want to talk about the situation; honestly, of course, but in a way that helps you manage the communications and the perceptions of what's happening.

  Be sure to consider the impact of your statements on all of your stakeholders. Choose your words carefully. You don't want anyone, especially your funders, to consider the organization unreliable or a bad risk. Express your concern and compassion, but don't admit or assign guilt. (A caveat: If your organization has obviously done something wrong, admit it, explain your plan for correcting the problem, and discuss how you will prevent a reoccurrence.) Present the situation realistically, without being overly emotional, and without blaming people. Don't make the situation look hopeless. Your reaction needs to be seen as appropriate, proportionate, and well thought out.

  Write down, and agree on, three versions of your official statement. These are used for different audiences and platforms – the short statement on Twitter, the mid-length one on Facebook, and the long one to the press, for example. (I usually start with a long version and edit down.) The written statement helps assure that your story is presented consistently, no matter who is speaking. This consistency helps your credibility.

  Distribute your approved statement to the Board and others designated to speak for the organization, and emphasize the importance of sticking to it.

- **Roll out your message.**
  Your plan should include rollout timing. What's the

priority of getting the information out on different platforms? This will differ depending on the situation, but it's important to pre-think so you can react quickly and precisely when you need to. Here are a few of the stakeholders that you will probably want to contact in almost any situation that you deem to be a crisis or emergency:

- Proactively contact local media, especially if they have already started to cover your story, and offer to talk with them as soon as possible. Chose journalists who will report accurately and don't have an axe to grind. Think about the impact of your language, and test it on a few people before you roll it out.

- Contact your major funders and supporters. Let them know what's happening. Provide the official statement and answer all of their questions. Do not wait for them to contact you.

- Reach out to your staff and make sure that they understand what's going on, what you're doing to deal with the situation, and how it's going to impact them. They rely on their jobs to pay the rent. It's only reasonable to let them know how their employment might be impacted, or not, due to the situation. Be sure they know who the official spokesperson is and that they should refer all questions to her.

- Your social community will want to know what's happening. As you probably have noticed, bad news travels fast. You may be surprised at how quickly you start getting calls and emails from concerned stakeholders. These can include your clients, your vendors, and anybody you interact with. So be sure that you're ready to get your information out through social media, including the possibility of an email blast.

- Any other stakeholders that haven't been covered need to be reached with your consistent messaging.

- **Be alert and be nimble.**
  Your planning should acknowledge the fact that you can't plan for everything. Any crisis situation can change rapidly. You need to be ready for that change and ready to adapt to it. New information may mean that you need to change your messaging or that you need to reach out a second time to the media or stakeholders. In any crisis, be ready for rapid developments, and be prepared to act quickly as the situation changes. If negative messaging occurs on social media or newspapers/TV, be sure to address it and get the accurate story, i.e. your thought-out messaging, to those individuals. Do not let their negative messaging go unaddressed.

After the storm has passed

After your crisis has passed, you need to mop up. Contact your press list and other stakeholders again with information that summarizes what happened, who was affected, and how the organization dealt with the issues. Talk about measures put in place to prevent such a situation from happening again, or how the organization will be better prepared to deal with it in the future. Remember to include your staff, so that they understand what happened.

Finally, do a debrief with your leadership team and Board to examine how well your planning worked. Make the necessary changes to your overall crisis management plan and to your crisis communications plan. And remember – review these documents at least annually.

When all this is done, you've earned a time to relax and unwind. But don't get complacent. It could all happen again tomorrow.

22

How to Help Your Board Help You

In a well-run organization, the Board of Directors, Executive Director (ED), and staff are all on the same path, pulling in the same direction, working for the same goals, and speaking the same language. Here are some tips on how to achieve and maintain that in your organization.

As we've seen, organizations that embrace Systems Marketing enjoy coherent communications throughout the organization. Everyone on the Board and staff realizes that their speech and actions impact the perceptions of, performance, effectiveness, and sustainability of the organization.

The Board and Executive Director have to work in a close partnership to create and sustain a high-functioning organization. This partnership impacts the entire staff, including the folks responsible for marketing and communications.

Strategic Planning

That close partnership starts with the strategic planning process. Strategic planning takes a lot of work, but it is essential to provide direction and to empower everyone in the organization to be working toward the same goals, and speaking with the same voice. I'm not going to provide a strategic planning primer here, but will mention a few key items that your strategic plan needs to include.

Obviously, any strategic plan needs to include goals and timelines, personnel assignments, and budget considerations. However it's also important that your strategic plan include communications goals and methods that will support all the other efforts. Your strategic plan should include key messaging concepts, so that everyone in the organization is saying the same things about the work, mission, and impact. That's where your Board gets involved with the marketing communications efforts. Some Board members may have experience in marketing or communications and will be able to add useful insights and ideas to the strategic plan. The Board can be valuable thought partners in the MarCom messaging and methods conversation.

When I'm working on strategic planning, I like every goal and activity to include a communications and/or marketing component, so that the Board and the staff appreciate the importance of communications in the success of the organization. Regardless of the Board's expertise, you want them to be aware of the importance of communications in the success of the organization, and of the fact that communications is being built in. And of course, this bakes MarCom accountability into the strategic plan.

As an example, you might plan to issue a press release every quarter, add Twitter and FaceBook to your marketing mix, and post pictures of all your events on Pinterest. Your plan will include these specifics, as well as goals for impact and frequency of reporting on that impact. In addition, you may assign these duties as part of the plan. With some luck, you may get one or more Board members to agree to provide regular contributions, perhaps once or twice a year.

Board/Staff Interaction

Some organizations frown on staff interacting directly with the Board, but I think it's a good idea. It's especially good for the marketing people to be in touch with members of the Board who have experience in marketing. It's also important to leverage the Board's connections and contacts for marketing communications purposes, especially when it comes to fundraising, and ultimately, in many activities. It may very well be that certain Board members know people with areas of expertise that are going to help the marketing and communications of the organization. They may also have connections that can directly impact the success of a campaign or program. Having all this communication filtered through the Executive Director can be a waste of her time – but don't ever try to cut your ED out of the conversation. In addition, be aware of the value of your Directors' time. You don't want to overstay your welcome by bothering the Board members too often. And of course, some are going to be more open to conversations than others.

When I've interacted with our Board members it's been with very particular questions. I always start by making sure the person I'm calling or emailing has time and is interested in the project that I'm asking their assistance with. If it's a phone call, I always start by asking, "Do you have a minute?" In email, I am brief and to the point, and always include a subject line that is descriptive of what I'm going to be asking about.

Questions I have asked Board members are typically in these categories:

- I have an idea for a new product/program. What you think?

- We'd like to reach someone in a particular organization. Do you know someone there?

- I'm planning a campaign and I've written up a description. Would you mind looking at it and commenting?

I found that when I'm respectful of Board members' time and expertise, they're happy to help.

Here are the best ways to make ensure that you and your Board have a good working relationship:

1: Be brief and to the point.

2: Be clear in your communications.

3: Be respectful of the Board members' time.

4: Be aware of the Board members' areas of expertise.

5: Don't go to the Board too often.

23

Helpful Resources

No list of this sort can be complete. New resources become available every day, and yet, some old books are still the best source on their subject.

This list comprises some of my favorite sources of marketing and nonprofit information. I think you'll find many of them useful, and some career-changing.

Starting a nonprofit

There are a countless opinions on starting nonprofit organizations. Here are some resources I like.

Nolo Press: How to Form a Nonprofit Corporation in California. http://www.nolo.com/products/how-to-form-a-nonprofit-corporation-in-california-non.html. Highly recommended. Includes all the forms you need. Versions for other states are available.

How to Start a 501c3 Nonprofit Organization: http://www.wikihow.com/Start-a-501c3-Nonprofit-Organization. More than just the legal stuff. Provides a lot of good tips.

Grantspace: How do I start a nonprofit organization? http://grantspace.org/topics/starting-a-nonprofit. Also good.

And of course, you had better understand the tax implications of your choices. Visit this IRS section for more information on tax considerations: http://www.irs.gov/Charities-&-Non-Profits.

Books on marketing

These are some of my favorites. Most of these are a few years old. I find that only 1-2% of business or marketing books are really worth the paper they are printed on or the electrons that display them. These books have actual, useful information. While the media has changed, the basic thinking behind marketing decisions remains remarkably non-perishable. Many of these books and authors have associated websites that you can easily find using your favorite search engine.

Selling the Invisible, Harry Beckwith, 1977, Warner Books

Direct Mail Copy That Sells, Herschell Gordon Lewis, 1984, Prentice Hall

Guerilla Marketing, 4th ed., Jay Conrad Levinson, 2007, Houghton Mifflin

Romancing the Brand, David N. Martin, 1989, American Management Association

How Brands Become Icons, Douglas B. Holt, 2004, Harvard Business School Publishing Corporation

MaxiMarketing, Stan Rapp and Tom Collins, 1987, McGraw Hill

Some useful websites

This category changes fast, but I think these links will endure. There are literally thousands of marketing and communications websites out there, but here are a few that I like to help you get started.

www.Linkedin.com has many groups for people working the non-profit sector, including some on marketing and fund raising.

www.Facebook.com also has a lot of good organization pages and discussions.

www.guidestar.org provides information on almost every US nonprofit.

Free QR code generator: http://qrcode.kaywa.com/

Survey Monkey is one of my favorite online survey sites. www.Surveymonkey.com

Google Analytics are essential for measuring online impact: www.google.com/analytics

Google.com is still one of the best places to start any sort of research. Check out the specialized search tools in the "Even More" menu. Other search engines offer similar tools.

www.VerticalResponse.com is one of the better emailing services. I like them because they offer free accounts to nonprofits.

And, if you need more of my bon mots, or want to contact me, please visit my website, www.BenDelaney.com.

And also...

Here are a couple more useful resources that can help you improve your writing. If you want to write well, have these by your desk.

The Elements of Style, Fourth Edition, 1999, William Strunk Jr. and E. B. White, Longman

The Associated Press Stylebook, 2013, Associated Press, Basic Books

Your Nonprofit Marketing Glossary

Like any field of specialization, nonprofits and marketing have their own peculiar jargon. When you combine the fields you get more terms of art. Because no one is born knowing all of these arcane terms, let me offer definitions of some of the most common. Acronyms follow the glossary.

Above the fold: Appearing above the bottom of the viewer's screen. This is an old newspaper term referring to what one saw when the newspaper was on a stand; everything above the horizontal fold was visible.

Accountability: Being responsible for your promises. This means that people do what they say they will do, or that vendors deliver what they promise, or that programs will be planned with measurable goals and evaluated frequently.

Advertising: Published promotional messages, often requiring payment for placement.

Audience: Everyone you're sending a message to. *Save the Kittys'* audience would be, in part, cat lovers.

B2B: Business to Business. Used to discuss types of marketing and business models.

B2C: Business to Consumer. Traditional advertising and retail businesses.

Brand, Branding: The perception of your organization in the minds of your audience members. Branding is the act of creating a Brand impression.

Broadcast: Widely dispersed, often via radio waves. Traditionally, radio and television. Now includes satellite and cable companies.

Case Statement: An explanation of why the organization does the work it does. This should help donors understand why their help is important.

Collateral: Literature and other printed materials used as an adjunct to marketing and sales efforts.

Conversion: Changing the status of a contact from interested to buyer. At a conference, you might collect a lot of business cards. Those who actually buy something or donate something, are considered converted.

Direct Response: Any form of promotion that is sent directly to particular people or organizations, and which includes a vehicle to enable response to the sender.

Elevator pitch: A fifteen to thirty second presentation of your organization or product, intended to start a more in-depth conversation.

Evaluation: Measuring results against expectations.

Five W's: Who, What, When, Where, Why. The basic foundation of a good story.

Hash Tag: The "#" symbol placed in front of a word on social media sites such as Twitter or Facebook. It is used like this: #NPMktngBook.

Hits: The number of pages requested from your web server. Note that each visitor may make many requests, so hits and visitor count are distinctly different.

Impact: In the nonprofit world, typically the difference you make in relation to your cause. A workforce development organization might measure impact in terms of clients obtaining paid work.

MarCom: Marketing and Communications. A common term for the combination of traditional marketing and public relations.

Market Research: Research done to understand or evaluate a particular marketing question, such as: how many units of this product can I expect to sell, why do people donate to our organization, or how do other organizations like ours raise funds.

Marketing Mix: The combination of marketing tools and techniques being used to address a particular marketing requirement.

Mission Statement: An official statement of what an organization exists to do.

Nth Name Selection: Selecting a random portion from a mailing list by selecting every nth name. For example, to obtain a 10% sample of a 10,000 name list, one would chose every 1,000th name. Typically used for testing a mailing list.

Online: Found or placed on the Internet. Websites, email and direct messaging are all online technologies.

Outdoor: Billboards, busses, trains, transit shelters, etc. Typically, refers to advertising placed in those locations.

Pay per Click (PPC): Online advertising that is paid for in direct relationship to the number of people clicking through to a destination, such as a website. Typically, advertisers pay a set amount for each click.

Positioning: Messaging, graphics, and placements that create perceptions of your brand in the mind of the audience that reflect how you wish to be perceived. A vital part of branding.

Print: Printed materials. Often used to indicate magazine and newspaper advertising, but can also mean direct mail pieces, brochures and other printed promotional material.

Promotional items: Pens, t-shirts, memo pads and other items imprinted with the sponsor's name. Sold or used as gifts that help people remember the sponsor.

Response Rate: The portion of the audience for a marketing effort that responds to it. Also the pace at which responses are received.

Return on investment (ROI): What you get back on an investment. Remember, you don't only measure money. The Social Return on Investment (SROI. see below) is equally important to nonprofits.

Search Engine Marketing (SEM): Using search engine results for advertising

Search Engine Optimization (SEO): Various techniques for the design and content of a website that are intended to improve results in search engines.

Social Media: Online media that connect people directly or through affinity groups. Twitter, Facebook, Google+, and LinkedIn are well-known social media.

Social Return on Investment (SROI): The social benefits, as opposed to monetary benefits, of an effort compared to its cost.

Stickiness: The characteristics of a website that encourages visitors to spend extended time on the site.

Sustainability: The ability to continue operations. Often, this means raising enough money to offset expenses. An important gauge of a nonprofit organization's durability.

System Marketing™: Ben Delaney's system of marketing that includes every staff member, every activity, and every communication, in a unified messaging environment.

Tag Line: A slogan or motto, typically used with a logo, to help identify an organization or strengthen its brand.

Test: In marketing, trying several methods, media or audiences to determine which respond best to a particular offer, method of communication, or product.

Transit: Describing advertising on and in busses, taxis, trains, boats, and their terminals.

Unique Sales Proposition (USP): The distinct and different sales argument that only one brand can make.

Vision Statement: The statement of what an organization believes will happen due to their activities. Typically presented with the Mission Statement and Case Statement.

Acronyms used in this book

B2B	Business to Business	**ROI**	Return On Investment
B2C	Business to Customer	**SEM**	Search Engine Marketing
CPM	Cost Per Thousand		
ED	Executive Director	**SEO**	Search Engine Optimization
FAQ	Frequently Asked Questions	**SOP**	Standard Operating Procedure
FP	For Profit	**SROI**	Social Return On Investment
NP	Nonprofit		
PPC	Pay Per Click	**USP**	Unique Selling Proposition
PR	Public Relations		
PSA	Public Service Announcement	**XML**	eXtended Markup Language
QR	Quick Response [code]		

About the Author

Ben Delaney provides organizational leadership and consulting at a strategic level. Over thirty years of executive leadership, marketing, serial entrepreneurship, and evaluation enables him to enhance the effectiveness of mission-driven organizations and social enterprises.

Ben leads and collaborates on teams that enhance the mission, values, culture and impact of organizations that serve the community and the world. He has had top executive responsibility in organizations showing consistent growth and triple bottom line impact. He considers mentorship and team development essential aspects of leadership.

Ben focuses on several areas of significant impact:

- Effective marketing and communications as part of every nonprofit's strategy for success.

- Use of business best practices to further social and beneficial causes.

- Social enterprise and Corporate Social Responsibility.

- Evaluation, especially building evaluation into new programs.

- Leveraging strengths through collaboration and partnership.

Ben's background includes business management, strategic planning, marketing, research, publishing, systems analysis, computer programming, and writing. His clients have included dozens of Fortune 500 companies and many universities and government agencies, in more than a dozen countries.

With over 100 articles and three books in print, Ben is a well-respected observer of marketing, technology, and the interface between technology and human activities. He has appeared frequently on television and radio, has been cited in major publications around the world, and has won multiple awards for marketing and writing. His presentations, both in America and abroad, are consistently highly rated.

Ben served on the Board of the San Francisco Bay Area Chapter of the Social Enterprise Alliance and was President of his local neighborhood association. He has served as Executive Director of two nonprofits. He lives in Oakland, California.

Ben is available to help your organization succeed. As a dynamic speaker or as an advisor to your leadership team, he enjoys helping nonprofits succeed. You can contact him through his website, www.BenDelaney.com or by emailing NPMH@BenDelaney.com.

Index

Please note that generally, plural forms are indexed with the singular.

B

CPSIA information can be obtained
at www.ICGtesting.com
Printed in the USA
LVHW071139110819
627236LV00020B/1030/P